CHERISHED MEMORIES

By

Smt. T.R. Kanakammal

Translated from Tamil by
Smt. Lalitha Krithivasan

SRI RAMANASRAMAM
Tiruvannamalai
INDIA
2002

Cherished Memories — English (Tamil original: **Ninaivil Niraindavai** by Smt. T.R. Kanakammal) Translated by Smt. Lalitha Krithivasan. Published by V.S. Ramanan, President, Sri Ramanasramam, Tiruvannamalai 606 603. India Tel: 91-4175-37292 Fax: 91-4175-37491 Email: alagamma@vsnl.com Website: www.ramana-maharshi.org

ISBN No: 81-88225-21-5

Price: Rs 90
CC No: 1045

Designed and typeset at
Sri Ramanasramam

Printed by
Aridra Printers
Bangalore 560 003
Phone: 3346025

PUBLISHER'S NOTE

Those who have basked in the presence of Bhagavan Sri Ramana Maharshi are truly fortunate. They are to be revered, for they swam in the ocean of Sri Ramana's Grace that is everflowing, regardless of time and space. These devotees have come forward to share the experiences they have had in the physical presence of Sri Bhagavan with other devotees. These reminiscences of old devotees, in recent years, have taken the shape of books and are carrying the message and Grace of Sri Bhagavan all over the world.

"Cherished Memories" by Smt. Kanakammal is unique in more than one sense. Though 'young' in the list of old devotees of Bhagavan Sri Ramana, her memories are green and fresh and are capable of transporting readers to the presence of Bhagavan as also to those times. Her memories also include the experiences and accounts of Muruganar, a staunch devotee of Sri Bhagavan as she had the opportunity of serving him for many years. Thanks to the efforts of V. Ganesan, these memories are on record and are part of the Ashram publications now.

Sri Bhagavan is pure like crystal. As crystal reflects the various colours in front, the devotees' various modes of expression of devotion are reflected in Sri Bhagavan. They also serve as a guide to other devotees to adopt the highest spiritual path as expounded by Sri Bhagavan. "Cherished Memories" of Smt. Kanakammal will be of great help to us and we are deeply indebted to her for her effort.

14th January 2002   PUBLISHER
Makara Shankaranti Day   SRI RAMANASRAMAM

PREFACE

The glory of 'Temple Worship' is that it accommodates the various moods of the devotees. The main deity (*moola murti*) represents the 'Still' nature of the Lord while the processional deity during festivals (*utsava murti*) represents the 'Action' (Shakti) aspect.

For the devotees of Bhagavan Sri Ramana Maharshi, the main deity is "Sri Ramaneswara Mahalingam" enshrined on the southern slope of Arunachala Hill in Sri Ramanasramam. This 'Moola Murti' is the beacon light for those who want to escape the ocean called 'samsara'. Those who have *darshan* of Sri Ramaneswara Mahalingam are fortunate indeed.

The main deity beckons devotees to the inner sanctum to bless them. The 'Utsava Murti' seeks out devotees and blesses them at their door-step. The vast literature on and by Sri Ramana Maharshi, truly represent this aspect. Ramana literature has spread to all corners of the world, bestowing His Grace and destroying the ego of the devotees.

One of the rare souls living in our midst is Smt. Kanakammal, who basked in the gracious presence of Sri Ramana Maharshi. It is fortunate that she is narrating her personal spiritual experiences even now to earnest seekers. Her self discipline and spiritual memories are soaked in the devotion of Sri Bhagavan. For long years she remained a light within the bushel and now at the earnest request of devotees she has come forward to share her spiriutal wealth in the form of her commentaries (in Tamil) for 'The Collected Works of Sri Ramana Maharshi' as also her reminiscences.

How are we to repay our debt to Sri Bhagavan's devotees of yore for the priceless treasures they have shared with us? There is only one way i.e., to follow the path of "Self Enquiry", the royal path as shown by Sri Bhagavan. This 'Cherished Memories of Smt. Kanakammal' is also an aid to that Supreme path of 'Self Knowledge'. To aid us in this path I beseech the grace of Bhagavan Sri Ramana Maharshi.

V. GANESAN
SRI RAMANASRAMAM

CONTENTS

THE GENESIS OF THE BOOK

Sri Ramanasramam at the foot of the Annamalai Hill, served as the setting for several wonderful incidents. Every incident that occurred in Bhagavan's presence has an important lesson for all of us. Such lessons cannot be found in any book of philosophy. They are the priceless jewels locked away in the memories of those devotees fortunate enough to have witnessed them in person.

Bhagavan's answers to the queries of devotees eager to obtain clarifications on spiritual and moral matters constitute invaluable lessons for all spiritual seekers. These questions and answers were recorded by various devotees, and these records serve as guides to successive generations of Ramana devotees. Bhagavan was not in the habit of giving discourses. His life itself was a lesson in spirituality. Every incident and every remark, however casual and spontaneous it might appear to be, serve to illustrate some great truth.

Devotees like Munagala Venkataramaiah, Devaraja Mudaliar, Suri Nagamma, Ramanananda Swarnagiri, Paul Brunton and Maurice Frydman have compiled their memoirs. They were privileged to witness several conversations and episodes. In addition to this, these devotees were all gifted writers and their books are not only informative but also highly enjoyable. While reading these books one gets transported to the very times when these incidents actually took place. My own humble effort at writing cannot be compared to the wonderful works of these great authors.

I came to stay in Ramanasramam in 1946. Even in those days I noticed several devotees keeping careful notes about everything that went on in the ashram. Somehow it never occurred to me to write down my own personal experiences and observations. I was content with filling my eyes and ears with Bhagavan's glorious form and enthralling words. I used to relive every moment spent in his company.

The decision to write this book was not a spontaneous one — it was prompted by circumstances. I had been explaining Bhagavan's

Complete Works to a small group of devotees. Once in a while I would narrate some anecdote or the other, just to illustrate a point. Sri Kunjuswami, Sri Ganesan and Smt.Anuradha, who made up the little group were fascinated by the various incidents I told them. They insisted that I should write down everything I had recounted to them. At first I was reluctant but they persuaded me to make the attempt. They argued that unless I wrote about my experiences they would remain confined to my memories and none could get the chance of benefitting by their study.

At last for the benefit of devotees I was convinced that it was Bhagavan's will that I should write a book. I consider myself extremely fortunate because while I was trying to find the right words to describe each incident my memories transported me back to the happiest period of my life. . .those glorious days spent in Bhagavan's presence! Time and space are no more than illusions and the mind has the power to transcend these illusory barriers.

Sri Ganesan has always been fascinated by the accounts of old devotees he had witnessed the interaction between Bhagavan and his devotees.

To him goes the credit of persuading and motivating me to record my cherished memories in a book. I hope that by Bhagavan's grace more and more devotees feel the urge to write about their own experiences so that people come to know more about enchanting Ramana.

T.R. KANAKAMMAL
SRI RAMANASRAMAM

1. THE GREATNESS OF ARUNACHALA

"You destroy the ego of those who meditate upon You in the heart, O Arunachala!"

— *Aksharamanamalai* by Sri Bhagavan.

The sacred name 'Arunachala', consisting of five syllables (A-RU-NA-CHA-LA), is worthy of constant remembrance and repeated chanting. The ego or the 'I-thought' of the person who thinks of this Name disappears completely. Such is the power of the Name. It is practically impossible to destroy the ego; but the very thought of Arunachala can erase the ego and grant Liberation. It is said that 'Liberation is assured for those who take birth in 'Kamalalayam' (Tiruvarur), for those who visit Chidambaram, for those who die in Kasi (Benares) and for those who merely think of Arunachala.'

Many saints have described the glory of Arunachala with great fervour. Saint Guhai Namasivaya pays a glowing tribute to Arunachala thus: "Arunachala beckons to those who are desirous of gaining Liberation. This is the Hill that grants the wishes of devotees without any reservation. This Hill takes complete possession of the hearts of its devotees." The rewards that are bestowed upon those who respond to the call of Arunachala are best described by the *Saivite* saint Thiru Jnana Sambandha (who himself received several priceless gifts including a pearl-studded palanquin, a ceremonial umbrella made of pearls and golden cymbals from the Lord Himself) in these words: "All the sins of those who worship Arunachala disappear without trace", that is, the devotees of Arunachala receive the invaluable gift of Liberation.

Appar sings, "Arunachala! You are the beginningless Beginning! You alone are the Supreme Lord!" Sundaramurthy Nayanar, who has the distinction of being considered the beloved companion of the Lord, says, "Those blessed ones who give up all physical desires and experience love for You alone, will certainly realize You, my Lord!" Manickavachakar, whose poems are like garlands of precious stones adorning the neck of the Lord praises Arunachala thus: "O Arunachala, my revered Father, I praise Thee! Your form is the limitless ocean of beauty which gladdens my eyes, and I praise Thee!"

In this way Arunachala has been praised by the great *Saivite* saints in their devotional poems. It is seldom that all the four great *Saivite* saints have sung the praises of the Deity in the same temple. Tiruvannamalai is one of these very few temples to have enjoyed this rare honour. In addition to this Tiruvannamalai has the unique distinction of being known as the 'place where *Jivanmuktas* abound'. Guhai Namasivaya, Guru Namasivaya, Virupakshadeva, Sivaprakasa, Deivasikamani Desika, Esanya Jnana Desika, Seshadri Swami and Bhagavan Sri Ramana Maharshi are but a few of the realized souls who chose Tiruvannamalai as their place of residence.

It is not only the great souls in mortal form who chose Arunachala as the venue for their penance and meditation. The Mother of the Universe, Parvati Devi Herself chose this spot for penance. The *Puranas* tell us how the Divine Mother came down to the earth to atone for a thoughtless prank She played on Lord Siva, as a result of which the entire universe was plunged in darkness for ages together. The Divine Mother performed penance in Tiruvannamalai and the Lord, pleased with Her devotion, appeared before Her and granted Her a half of His Form. She was desirous of everlasting union with Her Lord and therefore, He made Her an inseparable part of Himself. This is the story behind the manifestation of Lord Siva as Ardhanareeswara.

The *puranic* account of the appearance of the Arunachala Hill is very interesting. Brahma the Lord of Creation, became very conceited when he saw the beauty of his own creation. Vishnu the Preserver, was also quite proud of his own capabilities in taking care of the entire created universe. The point to be noted however, is that it was Brahma's arrogant and taunting actions that ignited the spark of pride in Vishnu. Brahma went to Vaikuntam (the abode of Vishnu) and boasted to him about his own prowess. He said, "If I had not created the Universe, how could you have looked after it? Don't ever forget that without me you would have been nobody. In fact, even now, I could remove you from here and create a new authority for this position. Have you forgotten that it was I who caused Rishi Brighu to curse you and thus created the opportunity for you to manifest yourself in the ten *avatars* (incarnations)? You should learn to give me the respect I deserve. Otherwise, I will create somebody new and take all your powers away.

Maybe you are under the impression that you are greater than I am just because I appeared from the lotus in your navel. Don't you remember that you manifested yourself in a stone pillar in response to Prahlada's prayers? Now, can I say that the stone pillar is your father just because you came out of it? Wouldn't that argument be quite ridiculous? Well, your idea that you are my father just because I came out of your form is as ridiculous. The forest fire that is kindled by the rubbing together of two dry twigs has the power to destroy the entire forest. In the same way, I who appeared to come out of you have the power to destroy you completely. If you are not convinced let me give you one more illustration. You know that the ears of an animal appear first and the horns, much later. Yet the horns are the powerful weapons, whereas the ears are worthless in a fight. Now do you understand how foolish it would be for you to think of yourself as my superior? You are not even my equal leave alone being superior!" Thus spoke Brahma in his pride and ignorance. What a fine illustration of the saying, 'pride goes before a fall'!

Incensed by Brahma's cruel teasing, Vishnu retorted, "He who insults his mother or his motherland, it is said, will certainly suffer for it. You seem to have forgotten the circumstances of your coming into being. Do not mistake my tolerance as a sign of weakness. I would prefer not to harm you as you are like a son to me. But if you exceed the limits of my tolerance I will not hesitate to destroy you. After all, did I not destroy Madhu and Kaitabha, even though they were my own sons? I can destroy you with equal ease. It is said 'he who planted the sapling will not cut down the tree.' But there is a limit to a father's tolerance. Do not force me to be harsh. Be careful what you say and do, otherwise you might land yourself in great trouble.

Actually, I find your arrogant bragging quite amusing. Maybe you have forgotten what happened when you annoyed Lord Siva. You were under the impression that just because you had five heads like Him your power was also equal to Lord Siva's. So you went to Him and irritated Him with your arrogant behaviour. And what happened to you then? Lord Siva plucked off one of your five heads. Could you do anything about that? You who boast about your prowess at creating limitless worlds and numerous life-forms, were you able to create a new head for yourself? Of course not! When you cannot even create a single new head and that too, for your own benefit, how can you consider yourself invincible or superior to all others?"

Vishnu continued, "Have you also forgotten your encounter with the demon Somukasura? You came rushing to me when he threatened you. Now, why did you do that? If you were really as powerful as you claim to be, why should you have needed my help? You were incapable of retrieving the Vedas from the wicked Somukasura and I had to take my *Matsya Avatara* (Fish Form) and chase him to the bottom of the ocean, fight him, kill him, and get the Vedas back. What makes you think I am not powerful enough to kill you also just the way I killed Somukasura? I admit that I have no real wish to kill you, but if you persist in your foolish taunting, I might lose my patience and destroy you in a fit of anger. So, do not provoke me further."

It is a well-known fact that the faults of a loved one go largely unnoticed. But when love has gone, every little thing gets magnified and every small disagreement gets blown out of proportion. The debate between Brahma and Vishnu which was just a verbal duel in the beginning, soon led to more and more heated arguments until finally, it became a full-fledged battle. Who can withstand the fury of the gods? When the Creator and the Preserver of the Universe were engaged in battle, all of creation suffered. There was utter chaos everywhere. At last, it became so terrible that the *devas* (celestial beings) could not bear it any longer. They went to Lord Siva and begged Him to intervene.

Lord Siva knew the reason for the rivalry between Brahma and Vishnu. He could have easily put an end to the disagreement by displaying His limitless power. But He chose to achieve this in a different way.

As Brahma and Vishnu were busy fighting, they suddenly saw an endless column of fire that had manifested beside them. The primal sound of the Pranava *mantra* (OM) filled the air. Brahma and Vishnu marvelled at this sight and paused to consider the origin of this awesome phenomenon. Soon, it occurred to them that this marvellous manifestation could serve a practical purpose in settling their dispute. They decided that they should find the limits of the seemingly endless column of divine light. Whoever could reach one of the ends of the column, they decided should be considered superior to the other.

As soon as this decision was reached Brahma took the form of a swan and flew upwards, determined to reach the top of the column. This is what the *Sivapuranam* says about Brahma's actions: "Brahma, who could recite the four Vedas simultaneously with his four mouths and is the lord of the Goddess of Knowledge, took the form of a bird. Does this not tell us how badly he was affected by the rise of his ego?" We refer to a stupid person as being 'bird-witted'. Do we not? The poet points out the irony of the wisest of the gods taking the form of a bird and flying off on a mission unworthy of his position. This would never have happened if he had kept his mind under control.

Meanwhile, Vishnu had taken the form of a boar and started digging into the earth hoping to find the root of the column. Vishnu, the mighty God who had measured the three worlds with three footsteps was now burrowing into the earth. When referring to someone who has lost his high status do we not say, 'He has fallen into the depths'? Vishnu was now intent upon pushing himself more and more deeply into the very bowels of the earth. The lesson to be learnt from this incident is that when the ego is allowed to assert itself, even the greatest being starts behaving in a petty manner.

Brahma, who had set out to locate the summit of the column, flew on and on for years together, but however high he flew, he was no nearer his goal. He was tiring fast. The feathers in his swan-body were dropping off one by one. He was very close to despair and had almost decided to abandon his fruitless quest when he saw a *Ketaki* flower dropping downwards. Brahma asked the flower, "Where are you coming from?" The flower replied, "I slipped from Lord Siva's crown and have been falling for a few thousand years. As yet I have not got even a glimpse of the bottom of this column. I am growing quite tired. Please move aside and let me pass. I would be glad to get to the end of my journey." The flower's words gave Brahma an idea. He said to the flower, "I have just come from the earth and I will carry you down to the bottom with me if you agree to do a small favour for me." The flower, being close to exhaustion, was only too happy to get a lift to the earth. So it agreed to do what Brahma wanted it to do. Brahma made the *Ketaki* flower promise to support his claim that he had himself travelled to the top of the column of fire and plucked the flower directly from the top. Now Brahma was certain that he could easily convince Vishnu to concede that he had won the contest. He hurried downwards with the flower in his hands, rejoicing in his triumph.

In the meantime, Vishnu was going deeper and deeper into the earth's core, but the column of fire seemed to go on for ever. Soon, Vishnu realised that he could never hope to find the root of the column. He decided to return to the surface and admit his inability to reach the goal. In this lies Vishnu's greatness. Though he was as guilty as Brahma in his original pride, he proved himself superior to Brahma when he realised his limitations and determined to admit as much.

When Vishnu reached the surface of the earth, Brahma rushed up to him and said, "Now you know which one of us is superior. I reached the top of this column just as I said I would. This column is indeed a manifestation of Lord Siva, for I saw His matted locks at the top of the column. Look, I have even brought you a flower which I plucked from His crown." The *Ketaki* flower confirmed Brahma's story.

The very next instant the column exploded and Lord Siva appeared before them. "Brahma!" thundered the Lord, "Your claims are fantastic indeed! Really, your words amuse Me!" The laughter of Siva shook the seven worlds and the whole creation trembled in fear. Brahma realised the extent of his foolishness. Trembling, he fell at the feet of the Lord.

Vishnu, too, prostrated to the Lord and sang His praises with utmost humility and devotion. Lord Siva was pleased with Vishnu's devotion and granted him several boons. Then He turned to Brahma and cursed him saying, "You shall no longer be worshipped as a god. There shall be no temples for you on this earth." The Lord cursed the *Ketaki* flower also. He ordained that the *Ketaki* would no longer be considered worthy of being offered to Him in worship.

Brahma overcome by shame, threw himself at Lord Siva's feet and begged His forgiveness. He cried, "O my Lord! Nobody can hope to know Thee fully. Ignorant creature that I am, I aspired to reach the very summit of Thy effulgent form. As soon as my ego raised its head my judgement was clouded and I set off on my foolish errand. My delusion and my arrogance prompted me to take the form of a small bird. Isn't that itself a sure proof of the fact that arrogance can only lead to humiliation?"

Though neither Brahma nor Vishnu had considered it at the time, Vishnu's task was by far the more difficult. He had set out to reach the source of the column of fire, that is, the feet of the Lord, which have more power than even His crown. Whereas the desire to rise higher and higher (ambition) often results in utter ruin, humility and the urge for total surrender at His feet can raise the seeker to great heights.

The main reason for Brahma's arrogance was his belief that, as he was the Lord of Saraswati (the Goddess of Learning), he must be the wisest of all beings. Saraswati is said to be seated on the tongue of Her Consort and this was the reason for Brahma's pride. As for Vishnu, the root of his pride lay in his being the Lord of Lakshmi, the Goddess of Wealth. The pride of wealth and the pride of intellect are the two most dangerous weaknesses. Of these, intellectual pride is by far the deadlier. Wealth can be measured and therefore the pride of wealth has its limits. But intellectual pride does not recognise any such limitations. Intellect, being intangible, defies measurement and does not allow comparisons to be made. This is why tests of intellectual prowess between scholars often prove inconclusive. The pride of intellect is so vicious that it urges its victim to seek glory at all costs tempting him to adopt foul means if fair ones prove ineffective. Did Brahma not resort to falsehood just to avoid facing defeat in the competition? And what is worse he even corrupted the *Ketaki* flower.

Our *puranas* contain various stories and parables. Our forefathers wanted to instil in us a strong sense of values. To this end they composed the *puranic* stories, each of which illustrates some moral. This particular story paints a very vivid picture of the consequences of pride. When ordinary men fight, we tend to dismiss the episode as only 'normal'. But when the same situation is presented with gods as central characters, the impact is much stronger and so the lesson proves more effective.

From this story, it is very clear that however high a person's status might be, the instant he allows his ego to assert itself, he topple down to the very depths of indignity.

Sri Muruganar has composed a song based on this *puranic* story. The song is titled *Arunachala Tattvam* (*Collected Works of Ramana Maharshi*) and it says, "The sudden rise of the blazing column of light in front of Brahma and Vishnu and their utter distress at not being able to know the same is symbolic of the *sphurana* of the heart centre as the real Self of the intellect and the ego."

The Arunachala Hill is said to have been a hill of fire in the *Kritayuga*, to have glowed as a ruby in the *Tretayuga*, as a hill of copper in the *Dwaparayuga* and a hill of stone in the *Kaliyuga*. Upto the beginning of the *Kaliyuga* the Hill had maintained the red colour of fire. The rocks in the Arunachala Hill are of great antiquity. The *Vairakkunru* near this hill is full of stones which are considered eminently suitable for sculpting the idols of Gods and Goddesses. The *Valluvar Kottam* in Madras has been built with stones taken from *Vairakkunru*. Bhagavan's sofa at Ramanasramam is also made of this stone and it bears testimony to the strength and beauty of the stone.

The *Arunachala Mahatmyam* records the origin of the Hill (*Collected Works of Ramana Maharshi*) in these words, "That day on which the ancient and wonderful Linga of Arunachala took shape is the asterism of *Ardra* in the month of *Mrigasira*. And the day on which Vishnu and the other *devas* worshipped the Lord in the form of effulgence is the day of *Maha Sivaratri*."

It also records Lord Siva's decree which says, "I ordain that residence within a radius of three *yojanas* (30 miles) of this hill shall by itself suffice to burn off all defects and effect union with the Supreme (even in the absence of initiation)."

According to the *puranas*, there are eight great Hills which are sanctified by the fact that God dwells on them. They are: Himalaya, Mandara, Kailasa, Vindhya, Nishada, Hemakoota, Neelachala and the Gandhamadanam. While these Hills are dwelling places of the Lord, the Arunachala Hill is Siva Himself! The Hill is not a separate entity but the manifestation of His Form. It is customary to place an idol of Nandi-Deva facing the main Deity in any temple of Lord Siva. In Tiruvannamalai we can see several idols of Nandi-Deva installed at various spots around the Arunachala Hill facing Him from many different angles.

Arunachala Hill is one majestic Sivalinga. The unique feature of the Sivalinga is that it can be said to have a form, but at the same time it is formless (*roopa-aroopam*). That is, the Sivalinga does have a shape, but this shape does not represent anything in particular. We recognise the Linga as a manifestation of Lord Siva. Yet, the Linga does not bear any resemblance to the form of any God or Goddess. In this respect it is like the Pranava (OM) which is pure sound alone. It is the primeval sound, apparently without any meaning, yet pregnant with meaning.

The greatness of Arunachala has been proclaimed in *Arunachala Mahatmyam*. Bhagavan has conveyed this in mellifluent and moving Tamil verses. One of these verses says, "That is the holy place! Of all Arunachala is the most sacred! It is the heart of the world! Know it to be the secret and sacred Heart-centre of Siva! In that place he always abides as the glorious Aruna hill!"

2. ARUNACHALA AND THE SAGE OF ARUNACHALA

The title of this chapter seems to suggest that Bhagavan and the Arunchala Hill are two separate entities. But if one were to study the life of Bhagavan, it would become clear that he never considered himself as being separate from the Hill. He considered the Hill as a manifestation of the Self. We could say that the Arunachala Hill had taken on a human form, the form of Bhagavan Sri Ramana Maharshi to spread the Divine Message among the common people of the world.

Bhagavan and the Arunachala Hill were one and the same. Bhagavan was always in a state of oneness with the Self (*Sahajatma Nishta*). To him, it was the most natural thing to carry on with everyday activities without ever wavering from that highest state of absorption in the Self. Numerous incidents in Bhagavan's life bear testimony to this fact.

In the last verse of the *Navamanimalai* (Necklet of Nine Gems), Bhagavan sings, "You are my Father and my Mother, You Who brought me into this world, O Arunachala!" Sometimes, Bhagavan would be gazing at something through the window in the hall. At those times, Bhagavan's gaze would be steady and unwavering. Once, a devotee asked Bhagavan, "What is it that You are looking at, Bhagavan? Is it the Light? Or is it Arunachaleswara?" To this query Bhagavan replied, "Is that what you want to know? I am looking at myself. There is after all nothing other than myself." Thus, Bhagavan has stated the essence of the theory of non-duality (*abheda-bhavam*) unequivocally.

After the Mother's passing away, Bhagavan would come down from Skandasramam everyday and spend some time near the spot where the Mother's mortal remains had been enshrined. One day Bhagavan came down as usual but did not return to

Skandasramam. The devotees came down looking for him. Upon finding him near the Mother's Samadhi they requested him to return to Skandasramam. But Bhagavan said "Some Power has brought me here. It was not my decision but the Divine Will." From that time onwards Bhagavan stayed in that spot at the foot of the Hill and Ramanasramam came up there.

At times, Bhagavan's words and actions would make us wonder whether he is a *bhakta* (devotee) melting with love for Arunachala rather than a dispassionate detached *jnani*. Once, during the Deepam festival, the deity from the temple was being taken in a ceremonial procession around the Hill. As the procession went past Ramanasramam, devotees of Bhagavan offered coconuts, flowers and fruits to the Lord and performed *Aarati*. Bhagavan was on his way to the cow shed at that time. Hearing the temple drums, he came and sat on the small bridge near the water tap. One of the devotees brought the *Aarati* plate with the glowing camphor which had been offered to Arunachaleswara. Bhagavan took the sacred ash from the plate and applying it on his forehead remarked softly, "The son is beholden to the Father." As he said this Bhagavan's voice was choked with emotion. His eyes glittered with unshed tears of ecstasy. This incident seems to illustrate the saying, "absolute Knowledge (*jnana*) is no different from absolute Devotion (*bhakti*)."

Bhagavan's love for Arunachala was so deep that he never left it even for a moment. He never tired of going around the Hill and visiting and revisiting his favourite spots on and around the Hill. He would sit for hours silently gazing at the peak of the Hill, totally enraptured by the sight. Every year, on Kartigai Deepam day, Bhagavan would gaze at the Hill through a pair of binoculars, his attention totally focused on the spot at which the sacred Deepam would appear.

The very mention of the name 'Arunachala' would bring a special glow to Sri Bhagavan's face. Bhagavan told us of the numerous miracles which took place on the Hill. He told us about his own life on the Hill, the various caves dotted all over the Hill, the greatness of the banyan tree on the northern slope of the highest peak, about the *Siddhas* who dwell on the Hill and about the priceless herbs that grow on it that cure even incurable diseases. He often remarked, "There is not a single spot on the Hill that my feet have not trod." To ordinary imperfect human minds and eyes, the Arunachala Hill seems to be made up of rocks and stones. But to Bhagavan, it was the manifestation of Divine knowledge, the embodiment of the Self. One should not forget that Bhagavan himself was the Arunachala Hill. This makes it even more remarkable — that he should be so fascinated by another manifestation of himself!

Bhagavan's adoration of the Hill is just one facet of the Master-Pupil relationship. Bhagavan is very eloquent in his praise of Arunachala. He often told his devotees that the Hill had elevated him from the level of an ordinary human being and shown him the way to union with the Self. Bhagavan's love and reverence for Arunachala are so great that his songs in praise of Arunachala have a special sweetness of their own. Bhagavan never tired of extolling the greatness of the Hill. On various occasions he has stated that Arunachala is the most potent manifestation of Lord Siva. In this connection, it would be pertinent to describe an incident that occurred while Bhagavan was staying in the Virupaksha Cave.

A *dikshitar* from Chidambaram having heard about Bhagavan, came to see him. He stayed in Tiruvannamalai Town and visited the Virupaksha Cave daily. During every visit, he had long, scholarly discussions with Bhagavan on various spiritual matters. This *dikshitar* repeatedly said, "Bhagavan! Chidambaram is one of the holiest places in South India. Is it not the *Akasalinga Kshetram* (where the Lord is in His Cosmic Form)? I implore You to visit this hallowed shrine at least once Bhagavan!" After this had gone on for a while, Bhagavan wrote something on a piece of paper and gave it to the *dikshitar*. It was a poem and when translated this is what it said, "In the court (of Chidambaram), Siva, though motionless by nature, dances (in rapture) before His Shakti who stands still. Know that in Arunachala He stands in His solemnity and She withdraws there into His unmoving Self (*Necklet of Nine Gems*, v.1)." Needless to say, the *dikshitar* never again tried to persuade Bhagavan to visit Chidambaram!

On summer evenings, Bhagavan would spend long hours reclining on an easychair in the veranda outside the hall, quietly gazing at the Hill. At such times, Bhagavan's face seemed to take on a special glow and his eyes shone even more brilliantly than usual, almost as though Bhagavan was marvelling at his own unique good fortune (being in such close proximity to the Arunachala Hill).

Arunachala is one of the holiest spots in India, a catalyst in the spiritual evolution of sincere souls. The number of sages who have lived in and around Arunachala is beyond count. In the early days of Bhagavan's stay in Tiruvannamalai, he was totally absorbed in the Self. He neither ate nor slept nor talked. In those days he tried to avoid disturbance by staying in the most secluded spots. During this period, he stayed in the Pathala Linga Cave, in Gurumoortham and in the Virupaksha cave. All these mark the Samadhis (shrines) of great sages. The remarkable thing is that, by choosing to grace them with his presence, Bhagavan brought added glory to these already hallowed spots.

Some of the sages of Arunachala are Virupaksha Deva, Guhai Namasivaya, Guru Namasivaya, Satguru Swami, Eesanya Jnana Desika, Deivasikamani Desika, Sivaprakasa and Seshadri Swami. This Arunachala Hill, which proved an irresistible attraction for various sages through the ages, claimed yet another unique prize. It was a young and innocent boy of school-going age, Venkataraman (Bhagavan Sri Ramana), the darling of his mother's heart. Though barely seventeen, the boy possessed extraordinary spiritual potential. Hitherto, Arunachala had been a powerful magnet drawing sages to Itself. No wonder, young Venkataraman proved an irresistible target for the Hill! How could Arunachala leave the chosen boy unclaimed? He, the Divine Hunter, spread His net with utmost care. He enticed the boy to Tiruvannamalai by causing His Name to be uttered in the child's presence sending a thrill down his frame. And once he reached Arunachala there was no question of going back! He was ensnared for life! The Divine Hunter had captured the soul of Venkataraman and devoured him fully in a trice. Henceforth, he had no separate existence as an individual; he had merged with the Perfect Being. Bhagavan himself has acknowledged this in one of his songs. He says, "I have discovered a new thing! This hill, the lodestone of lives, arrests the movements of anyone who so much as thinks of it, draws him face to face with it and fixes him motionless like itself to feed upon his soul thus ripened. What (a wonder) is this! Oh souls! beware of It and live!* Such a destroyer of lives is this magnificent Arunachala which shines within the Heart!" (*Eleven Verses to Arunachala,* v.10)

---

* *Alternatively:* Oh souls! Think upon It and be saved!

Arunachala not only drew the young boy to Himself, but performed yet another far more remarkable feat. Arunachala persuaded Bhagavan Ramana the sage who was beyond all worldly attachments to burst forth with a romantic and mystic poem, the *Aksharamanamalai*. This brings to mind the incident in Saint Manickavachaga's life where Lord Siva appears before him and asks him to sing a *kovai* (a Tamil poem composed in a unique metrical form). Similarly, Lord Arunachala took pleasure in making Sri Ramana sing the singularly lyrical poem, the *Aksharamanamalai*. Bhagavan composed the *Aksharamanamalai* in response to the specific request of his devotees who wanted to chant it while going around asking for alms. But the greatness of the song lies in the fact that the devotee's every need is fulfilled by the mere recitation of this potent poem.

In one of the stanzas, Bhagavan refers to Arunachala as an ocean of Grace in the form of a Hill (*Arunachala Pancharatnam*, verse 1). This might sound strange, but it is an indisputable fact that the Arunachala Hill though it looks like any other hill of rocks and stones, is the limitless Ocean of Grace, the Lord Siva Himself.

Bhagavan did not have any Guru in the conventional sense, i.e., he had no human Guru. But Bhagavan has clearly stated the identity of his Guru. In *Aksharamanamalai*, verse 19, Bhagavan says that Arunachala has wiped out all his faults and taken possession of him. The greatest error is said to be arrogance and the true Guru is one who destroys the ego of the disciple. Bhagavan says that Arunachala is the destroyer of his ego and acknowledges Him as his Guru. In another stanza (twentieth) of the *Aksharamanamalai* Bhagavan says, "Arunachala! There are many in this world who are on the look-out for easy prey. Their eyes are like sharp swords which can pierce through all the defences of an ordinary mortal. Please take me into Your care Arunachala, and protect me from such unscrupulous people." Here, the reference is to false 'seers' who with deceptive looks and cunning speech, try to ensnare the unwary seeker and lead him deeper and deeper into ignorance. Only the real Guru can show the way to light; the false ones only lead one into the darkness of the abyss.

Aksharamanamalai, garland of exquisite verses, mirrors all human emotions like love, humour, valour, anger etc. However, the dominant mood is *sringara* (love/romance). The romantic symbolism is evident throughout the work. The last verse in which Arunachala is requested to bestow His Garland (of Divine Grace) on Bhagavan and accept Bhagavan's garland (of verses) in return, is a direct reference to the most important ritual in marriage — the exchange of garlands between the bride and the groom. This exchange of garlands is symbolic of the joyful union of two human beings. Bhagavan is asking Arunachala to solemnise the union of the *jiva* (the individual soul) with the *Para* (the Almighty), resulting in everlasting Bliss.

In the first three stanzas of the *Arunachala Ashtakam*, Bhagavan says that even in his childhood the consciousness of 'Arunachala' was there, deep down in his heart. As a child, he says he did not know what the name 'Arunachala' actually meant, but he felt that the name stood for something very precious something beyond the reach of ordinary mortals. When a relative told him that 'Arunachala' was another name for Tiruvannamalai, he did not quite grasp the significance of the information. Within a while however, the irresistible Power of Arunachala drew Bhagavan to Tiruvannamalai. Having arrived at Tiruvannamalai, Bhagavan gazed awe-struck at the Hill and sang, "Arunachala at first sight, might appear to be an ordinary hill of rocks and stones. But what a wonderful Hill this is! Its powers can only be guessed at! Even the most learned scholar cannot estimate the Divine Power of Arunachala!"

In the second stanza, Bhagavan says, "You drew me unto Yourself Arunachala. Powerless to resist Your pull, I came to You. As I stood gazing at You, Your power worked a wonderful transformation in me. I pondered, "Who is it that is looking at this Hill?" and at once my 'I-sense' disappeared. I had no identity of my own any longer. You alone remained. So I could no longer say, "I saw the Hill." At the same time I could not say, "I did not see." How can I deny You, Arunachala! In olden times it was You who imparted the Ultimate Truth through silence. You who were Dakshinamoorthy then, have now taken on the form of the Arunachala Hill. Can the Truth that Dakshinamoorthy preached through silence be expressed in words! You are the embodiment of the Truth, Arunachala, You who stand before me as this great hill spanning the earth and the sky!"

In the third stanza Bhagavan says further, "So great is the power of this Hill that the very sight of it cleansed my heart and destroyed my ego. I lost my individuality and merged with the Self. I had imagined that Arunachala would have a form that I could clasp to my heart. But now I know that this great Hill is a manifestation of the Almighty. My journey to this place to see Arunachala the Omnipresent is like the journey undertaken by a man who travels all over the world to catch a glimpse of the sky! Having arrived here, I am like a doll made of sugar drowning in the ocean — I am completely dissolved in You; I have merged with You totally. When I ask myself 'Who am I?', I realise that I have no identity apart from You. You are the only Truth!"

3. ARUNACHALESWARA TEMPLE

The sacred temple of Arunachaleswara is one of the biggest temples in Tamil Nadu. It is a huge temple covering nearly twentyfive acres and is truly marvelous in its construction. The temple walls are so high that they seem to be touching the sky.

The eastern tower (*Rajagopuram*) of this temple is the tallest in South India. It is even taller than the tower of the big temple in Thanjavur. The tower of the Thanjavur temple is 216 feet tall, whereas the one in the Arunachala temple is 217 feet in height .This huge tower is the main entrance to the Arunachala temple .The entrance is 98 feet wide and 135 feet long.

This tower is so majestic in its appearance that it is easy to fancy that it is the entrance not only to the temple but to the whole of the Arunachala Hill itself. When one beholds the Arunachala Hill from this spot, the entire Hill seems to be beautifully framed by this doorway and it appears as though the temple walls enclose the whole of the Hill.

There are five corridors in this temple. All the idols show excellent craftsmanship. The idols which are taken out in procession during the temple festivals are of *Panchaloha* (an alloy of five metals). The vahanas (ceremonial mounts) are remarkable both in size and in beauty. Of special note is the huge silver Nandi or sacred Bull which bears the idol of Arunachala on the fifth day of the annual Deepam festival. Its beauty is beyond description. There is no other festival like it anywhere else in the world. Its majestic expression and the proud look in its large eyes are artistic marvels.

The *Panchabhuta Kshetras* (the sacred spots where Lord Siva manifested Himself in the form of the five elements) are Kanchipuram [or Tiruvarur (Earth)], Tiruvanaikkaval (Water),

Tiruvannamalai (Fire), Kalahasti (Air) and Chidambaram (Space). Of these, Tiruvannamalai is the spot where the Lord has manifested Himself in the form of Fire. This fact is borne out by the tradition of "Fire-walking" on the Aadi-pooram day.* Devotees walk on glowing coals laid out in front of the Goddess' shrines on this day. This is the only temple in South India where such walking on fire is done within the temple precincts. Another tradition unique to this temple is the burning of the effigy of Kama (the God of Love) within the precincts of the temple during the spring festival. Everywhere else, the burning of Kama is carried out only on street corners. The *sthala vriksha* (sacred tree) of this temple is Magizha.

One of the *gopurams* (towers) of the temple is known as the Vallala Raja Gopuram. This tower attained fame through its association with Sage Arunagirinatha. It was from the top of this tower that Arunagirinatha hurled himself to the ground with the intention of ending his life. Lord Subrahmanya held him in His arms and saved him from death. Having saved his life, Subrahmanya commanded Arunagirinatha to sing the sacred Tiruppugazh (a compilation of hymns). The Lord even supplied His devotee with the first word of the poem Himself. The idol of Lord Subrahmanya in this shrine with the Vallala Raja Gopuram is known as the Gopurathu Ilaiyanar. This tower was built by the king known as Vallala Raja who was a great devotee of Lord Siva. This king was childless and he prayed to Lord Siva to bless him with a son. So pleased was the Lord with the king's devotion that He Himself became the king's child for a while and took upon Himself the duty of

---

* The Deepam festival also signifies the fire aspect of Lord Siva, as on the tenth day a fire is lit on top of the Arunachala Hill.

performing the last rites of Vallala Raja after his death. For the past 600 years, the deity from the Arunachaleswara Temple is taken to the village of Pallikondapattu on the appropriate day (*Maasi Makham*) every year, and here the Lord performs the annual ceremony of the king.

All the idols in the Arunachala Temple have a reddish glow. This is because a greater proportion of copper has been used in the *Panchaloha* (the alloy of five metals) of which the idols are made. This seems to fortify the fact that Tiruvannamalai is the *Agni Kshetra* and the Lord is in His Fire form in this place. The Sivalinga in the temple is said to be a swayambhu linga (i.e. it was not made by man but is self created).

The *samadhi* (tomb) of Idaikkaadar, one of the eighteen *Siddhas* (Enlightened Ones), is in Arunachala. The temples associated with the *Siddhas* enjoy a greater fame in Southern India. The *samadhi* of Karuvoorar is in the Big Temple in Thanjavoor. In Marudamalai we find the *samadhi* of Pambatti *Siddha* and in Palani there is the *samadhi* of Bhoga. In Tirupathi, we find the *samadhi* of Konganar. The *Arunachala Purana* proclaims that Lord Siva Himself has manifested as Arunagiri Yogi in the Northwest of the Hill .

There is a 16 pillared hall in the first quadrangle of the temple. Here we can see the figure of Kambattu Ilaiyanar* carved on one of the pillars. This figure has a fascinating story behind it. One of the rulers of Tiruvannamalai was King Prabuda Devaraya. This king had a close friend called Sambandandan who was a very great devotee of the Divine Mother. Sambandandan enjoyed Her Grace to such an extent that he only had to think of Her Form for Her to appear before him. Sambandandan was very

---

* Kambam-pillar; Ilayanar-the younger one, i.e., Lord Subrahmanya.

jealous of Arunagirinatha's fame. He was just biding his time for a chance to discredit Arunagirinatha in the eyes of the king and the rest of the world. He eventually came up with an apparently foolproof plan. He went to Prabhuda Devaraya and said, "O King! Arunagirinatha claims to be a great devotee of Lord Subrahmanya. Let us test the power of his devotion. You know that I can make the Divine Mother appear before me any time I want. I would like to challenge Arunagirinatha to a contest. I undertake to make the Mother appear before you. Let us see whether Arunagirinatha can make Lord Subrahmanya manifest Himself before us. If I lose the contest, I will leave Tiruvannamalai with my family and will never return. Arunagirinatha also should agree to go away from Tiruvannamalai for good in case he loses the contest". The king being a good friend of Sambandandan, was convinced that this would be an interesting competition and so he sent for Arunagirinatha and informed him of the conditions of the contest. Arunagirinatha readily agreed and suitable arrangements were made.

On the day of the competition, a large crowd gathered in the Arunachala Temple. Sambandandan was the first contestant. He meditated upon the Divine Mother and requested Her to appear before the expectant gathering. She acceded to his request and came down to earth but She was visible to Sambandandan's eyes alone. The king could not have her *darshan*. Hence Sambandandan was defeated in the contest.

Next, it was Arunagirinatha's turn. He had to bring down Lord Subrahmanya and make Him appear before the king and his retinue. Arunagirnatha sang soulful poems in praise of the Lord and begged Him to make Himself visible to the gathering. But Lord Subrahmanya did not come. He could not come because His Mother was holding Him in a tight embrace. This was Sambandandan's doing. Unwilling to accept defeat in the competition, he had decided to resort to subterfuge. He had requested the Divine Mother to clasp Her Son in a tight embrace so that He would be unable to respond to Arunagirinatha's call. At first, Arunagirinatha was puzzled by the Lord's seeming indifference. Through God's Grace however, he soon realised what was happening. Now he had to think of a way to free Subrahmanya from His Mother's hold. The resourceful poet soon hit upon an ingenious plan. He prayed fervently to the peacock which is Lord Subrahmanya's Mount. The peacock was pleased with Arunagirinatha's prayers and decided to help him. It spread its colourful feathers and started dancing. The Mother's attention was momentarily diverted. Captivated by the peacock's dance She unwittingly slackened Her hold upon Her Son. Seizing His opportunity, Lord Subrahmanya slipped out of His Mother's grasp and hurried down to earth. Arunagirinatha was singing an exquisite song beseeching Subrahmanya to come dancing down on His peacock. Even as he sang, the huge gathering was wonderstruck by the vision of Lord Subrahmanya dancing on the back of a beautiful peacock which descended gracefully and came to rest on one of the 16 pillars in the hall. The king and his subjects were speechless with wonder. Even Sambandandan was at a loss for words! The Kambathu Ilayanar temple commemorates this incident.

Next to the Vallala Raja Gopuram is the 'Parrot Tower'. We can see the figure of a parrot on the first tier of this tower. There is an interesting story connected with this too.

Sambandandan was determined to remove Arunagirinatha from Tiruvannamalai somehow. To this end, he was always busy hatching some cunning plot or the other. On one occasion, he convinced Prabhuda Devaraya that it was necessary for the king to obtain a flower from the Divine Parijatha tree. This tree grew only in Heaven and its flowers were said to be of incomparable beauty. The king commanded Arunagirinatha to get him a Parijatha flower at once. So, Arunagirinatha moved his spirit into the body of a parrot and in this parrot form, flew to Heaven. He plucked a flower from the Parijatha Tree and returned to earth with the flower in his beak. Meanwhile, the wicked Sambandandan had told Prabhuda Devaraya that Arunagirinatha was dead, and showed the king the lifeless body of Arunagirinatha. The king did not know that Arunagirinatha had only left his body temporarily to make use of the parrot's body for his trip to Heaven. In response to Sambandandan's urging the king ordered the immediate cremation of Arunagirinatha's body .

When Arunagirinatha returned to earth, he found that his human body had been destroyed. Therefore he was forced to stay in the body of the parrot. While in the parrot form, Arunagirinatha sang the beautiful *Kandar Anubhuti* in praise of Lord Subrahmanya. The figure of the parrot on the tower is in commemoration of the events recorded above.

Since the Arunachala Hill is Lord Siva Himself, the idol of the Lord that is kept in the Royal bedchamber in the Temple is in the form of a hill. The Deity is a *Sivalinga* atop a three tiered hill, which is a symbolic representation of the Sacred Meru Hill. This idol is unique to the Arunachala Temple. No other temple has an idol like this. The idol of Ardhanareeswara in this Temple (the Siva-Sakthi Form or the half God-half Goddess Form of the Supreme Being) is also a remarkably elegant work of art.

In every Siva Temple, we can see a figure of the Lingodbhava at the rear of the sanctum sanctorum. This figure is a symbolic representation of the form in which Lord Siva appeared before Brahma and Vishnu when they were trying to decide who was the more powerful. It was at Tiruvannamalai that Lord Siva manifested Himself as an endless column of fire and the Lingodbhava symbolises this event. Moreover, in every one of the hymns sung by the *Saivite* saint Tirujnanasambandar, the ninth verse is always dedicated to Arunachala. The saint has also composed many songs exclusively for the Lord of Arunachala. Devout Saivites chant, 'Annamalaikku Arohara' (Praise be to Annamalai), regardless of whichever Siva temple they happen to be in. But the reverberations of this soulful chanting on Arunachala is overwhelming according to Saiva Ellappa Navalar of the famed *Arunachala Purana*. In addition to this, all mendicants, whether in Tiruvannamalai or elsewhere, chant 'Annamalaikku Arohara' when they go around begging for alms.

Numerous festivals are celebrated in Tiruvannamalai every year. The most famous of these is the Deepam festival which falls in the Tamil month of Karthigai. This is a grand festival which stretches over a period of ten days. On the tenth day of the festival, a huge Deepam (Lamp) is lit at the top of the Hill. There is a large basin-like copper cauldron kept on the summit of the Arunachala Hill. This cauldron is filled with ghee and the lamp is lit at 6 o'clock in the evening of the tenth day of the festival. The light of this lamp is visible for a distance of nearly 30 miles in all directions. The practice of lighting a lamp at the top of the hill must have been in vogue from time immemorial. In the earliest Tamil literature, the phrase "Like a beacon on the top of a hill" is used as an illustration of widespread fame.

The origin of this tradition can be traced back to the legend of Ardhanariswara. According to legend, the Divine Mother Parvati came to Tiruvannamalai and did penance to be united with Her Lord. Lord Siva was so pleased with Devi's penance that He appeared before Her as a column of dazzling light and took Her into Himself. This merging of Siva and Sakthi is represented by the Ardhanaareeswara form. This event occurred on the full moon day under the star *Krithika* in the Tamil month of *Karthikai*. Ever since, it has been the practice to light a lamp at the top of the Arunachala Hill on this day every year and worship the Lord.

These ten days are marked by grand processions and other traditional festivities. The mounts of the deities are all of silver and each one is of remarkable beauty and size. The procession of the five main deities is an unforgettable sight. The Rishaba Vahana, or the sacred Bull, which carries Lord Arunachaleswara and His consort on the fifth day of the festival is worth special mention. This silver Bull is so huge that just watching the preparations for the procession is in itself an awe inspiring experience. Mounting the idols on the gigantic Bull and arranging the huge flower canopy are formidable tasks that require the utmost skill and care. When this magnificent Bull comes out of the temple bearing the idols of Lord Arunachaleswara and His Divine consort, the large crowd of devotees give it a rapturous reception. Witnessing this procession is an experience one can never forget.

When the Deepam is lit on top of the Hill, *Deeparadhana* (burning of camphor) is performed to all the five main deities within the Arunachaleswara temple. Simultaneously, the decorated idol of Lord Ardhanareeswara is brought out on a palanquin. It is as if the Divine Father and Mother are keen to shower their Grace upon the the crowd of devotees gathered there. Lord Ardhanareeswara comes out of the Shrine with the Bharani Deepam (ceremonial torch) showing the way and hurries along to the sound of drum beats. The other deities are already waiting for Him. He grants His *darshan* to everyone and in turn, He witnesses the Deepam glowing on top of the Hill. In case the Deepam is not visible due to rain or clouds on the top of the Hill, He paces restlessly to and fro, waiting for a clear view of the Deepam. Once He has seen the Deepam, He hurries back inside.

The Deepam festival is undoubtedly the grandest festival in Tiruvannamalai. Every year lakhs of devotees flock to Tiruvannamalai to witness the Deepam. It is believed that worshipping Lord Siva in His fire form on that day can grant liberation to the sincere devotee.

Another important festival is *Tiruvoodal* which takes place in January. Oodal means temporary estrangement or separation between lovers. This festival takes place on the second day of the Tamil month of *Thai*. The origin of this festival goes back to a very interesting legend.

Sage Bhringi (from Bhringa, a Sanskrit word for bee) was such an ardent devotee of Siva that he would not acknowledge any other god or goddess — not even Goddess Parvathi! Whenever Sage Bhringi went around Lord Siva and worshipped Him, he was particular to avoid Parvathi. So, when Goddess Parvathi merged Herself with Siva and appeared before the sage in the form of Ardhanareeswara, Bhringi took the form of a bee and, gnawing a hole through the Divine form, went around Siva's half of the form. This made Parvathi — who is Divine Energy — so angry that She withdrew all energy from Bhringi and reduced him to a mere skeleton. As this skeleton was too weak to stand, let alone continue his circumambulation, Lord Siva granted him a third leg to support himself. When Siva decided to go to Bhringi's hermitage in order to grant the sage liberation, Parvathi became very angry. She refused to accompany Siva to Bhringi's hermitage and rushed into the temple. Lord Siva found Himself in a very difficult position. His compassion for His devotee who was earnestly praying for liberation was so great that He was prepared to risk the displeasure of Parvathi. He decided to give *darshan* to Bhringi, thus granting him *moksha*. On His return from Bhringi's hermitage Siva pacified His Consort. The apparent division of the inseparable and the subsequent reunion are nothing but the Lord's Divine Sport. All these are depicted in a series of rituals in the *Tiruvoodal* festival.

4. BHAGAVAN SRI RAMANA MAHARSHI

In ancient times, Siva Himself was present here in His Divine form. Later He took the form of Fire which eventually turned into the Arunachala Hill. It is not possible for us to see the Divine form of Siva now in this modern age. It is said that Siva resides even now in one of the five peaks of the Hill as Arunagiri Yogi; again in a form that is invisible to the physical eye. As if to provide us all with an opportunity to see the Lord in human form, Arunachala drew the young Venkatraman from Madurai and made him stay at Arunachala. He stayed there as immovable as the Hill Itself, constantly showering his Grace upon innumerable devotees. It was as though Tiruvannamalai, already a sacred spot, had become further sanctified by the presence of Sri Bhagavan. It was through Sri Ramana Maharshi that the fame of Tiruvannamalai and Lord Arunachala spread far beyond the boundaries of India to the remotest corners of the world.

Bhagavan Sri Ramana Maharshi was born in a small village called Tiruchuzhi in South India and had his schooling at Madurai. In his childhood he was called Venkataraman. Even while he was a child, he used to have a constant continuous awareness (*sphurana*) of Arunachala. In later times, Bhagavan used to say that in his childhood, he believed that this kind of feeling was quite normal and common to all people. It was only much later that he realised that the feeling was not at all a common one. It was this constant *sphurana* resonating within, that drew him to Tiruvannamalai and kept him bound to the Arunachala Hill for fifty four years.

Bhagavan when he was young, somehow had the notion that Arunachala was something extraordinary, not within the reach of the common man. It was only when a relative returning from Tiruvannamalai explained it to him, that he realised that 'Arunachala' was another name for the place called Tiruvannamalai. The pull of Arunachala was irresistible and Bhagavan was drawn to the Hill just as inexorably as iron is drawn to a magnet. Once a devotee asked him, "Bhagavan, you have been gazing at the hill for such a long time. What is it that you are looking at?" To this, Bhagavan replied with a smile, "I am looking at my own Self."

Bhagavan was extremely simple in his appearance. Even in the coldest day of winter, he wore no more than a loin cloth. In the early days of his stay in Tiruvannamalai, he lived for a while in the Arunachaleswara temple. Whether it was within the Pathala Linga or under the Iluppai tree, Bhagavan had only a loin cloth to protect him from the elements. Even after the Ashram was established, Bhagavan never wore anything more. At times his devotees would beg him to use a shawl to cover himself but he would use it only occasionally to please them. He was indifferent to heat and cold. Even in the hottest hours of the summer days, he would remain bare foot, and would walk on the scorching rocks with measured steps in his usual graceful manner.

Bhagavan's simplicity was not confined to his appearance; even his teachings were amazingly simple and direct. Bhagavan was capable of conveying the most profound ideas in an uncomplicated way with a few beautifully chosen words. He taught not through words, but through his glorious life marked by extraordinary detachment and pregnant silence.

Once a visitor said to him, "Bhagavan, this is my first visit to the Ashram. I have been observing that people keep coming to you and asking questions and that you clear   all their doubts. I am so ignorant that I cannot even think of a question to ask you. How can I ever hope to be liberated?" The man was genuinely anxious and Bhagavan in his compassion told him, "You say you do not know anything. Who is it that is ignorant? If you can identify that person, you would realise the greatest truth. When one thinks that one knows everything, the ego becomes very strong and obstructs the path of realization. Is it not therefore better to think that one does not know anything?"

On another occasion, a lady who was visiting the Ashram for the first time said to Bhagavan, "Bhagavan, I have a desire. May I tell you about it?" Bhagavan asked her what she wanted. The lady replied, "Bhagavan, I want Realisation. That is my only desire. I have no other desires at all. All I want is realisation. Can you give me that?"

Bhagavan could hardly control his laughter. He said, "Yes, yes. That is very good." The lady was persistent. She said, "Bhagavan, please don't try to put me off with mere words. Please give it to me at once. Will you give it?" Bhagavan merely nodded his head. Finally the lady took leave of him. As soon as she left, Bhagavan burst into laughter. He said to the devotees around him, "Look at her! She is demanding Realisation and that too, immediately! Is it a parcel or a bundle that I can hand over to her as soon as she asks? She says she has no desire. Is this not a desire? When the mind is emptied of all desires, what remains is Realisation. This cannot be given by anyone. This has to be gained only through Sadhana."

Another of Bhagavan's devotees wanted to know how a *jiva* (individual) accumulated karma. Bhagavan replied, "First you must find out who this *jiva* is. After that you can start thinking about how it acquires karma. When you do not even know who or what a Jiva is, how can you determine whether it is affected by karma or not? These are unnecessary speculations. You should learn to turn the mind inwards. When this happens, all doubts cease and Realisation is achieved." In a few words, Bhagavan thus expounded the profound truth.

Bhagavan never professed himself to be a Maharshi. Neither did he acknowledge anyone as his disciple. If anyone asked for *Upadesa* (instruction), he would say, "Who is to instruct whom?" He used to say, "If I am a *Jnani* or a Realised soul, there cannot be any ignorant soul outside of me. On the other hand, were I not a Realised soul, there is no point in my giving instructions or Upadesa to anyone. Moreover, who is it that wants Upadesa? You must learn to seek him out, through self enquiry. That instruction which helps you in this quest is the real Upadesa." Though Bhagavan declined to function as a conventional Guru, his life itself served as a lesson to the sincere seeker. In each act of his life, there is a valuable lesson for us. The method of Self-enquiry does not make any distinction of age, sex, caste or creed.

5. WHO IS RAMANA?

Once, during a conversation with devotees, Bhagavan recounted an interesting incident involving Amrithanatha Yatindra. This is the story as narrated to us by Bhagavan:

"Amrithanatha was an unusual kind of person. He had a lot of interest in all kinds of things. From the early days of my stay in the Hill, Amrithanatha would visit me often. Sometimes, he would stay with me for a few days at a stretch. He wrote my biography in Malayalam. Once Nayana asked to have this book read out to him, but after listening to just a few chapters, he cried "Enough! Enough!" and tore the book to pieces! The trouble with Amrithanatha was that he liked to exaggerate. It was his practice to attribute all kinds of extraordinary qualities to the subject of his writings. His biography of me was also full of such exaggerated descriptions and this is probably what annoyed Nayana!

Once, while I was staying in the Virupaksha Cave, Amrithanatha came to see me. It was during this visit that he composed a poem in Malayalam, in which he tried to present me as an *avatar* (incarnation) of the Almighty. The song, when translated, would read: "The Ocean of Compassion, the great Seer, Bhagavan Ramana, who lives in the beautiful cave on the summit of the Arunachala Hill — who is he? Is he Vishnu? Is he the Preceptor of Lord Siva Himself or Lord Subrahmanya? Is he the great Sivayogi, Vararuchi? Or is he the greatest of all Seers, the incomparable poet Vyasa? My heart is full of eagerness to know the identity of my Master." Amrithanatha wrote this poem on a piece of paper and left it under my seat, while I had gone out. Leaving the poem there, he left the cave. When I returned to the cave, I found the piece of paper with the poem on it. After reading the poem, I wrote a reply also in the same metre as Amrithanatha's own composition. When he came back to the cave I gave my poem to Amrithanatha. The poem which I wrote in reply to Amrithanatha's queries, is as follows:

'Arunachala Ramana is the Supreme Being who sports within the lotus-hearts of all beings, beginning with Hari, in the form of Consciousness. If one enters, with a heart melting with devotion, the abode in which the Supreme Being is shining, his eye of knowledge will be opened and he will become Consciousness itself. The truth will become clear to him'. This song was later translated into Tamil also.

It was Amrithanatha's desire to attribute some super-human qualities to me. By asking, 'Is Ramana Hari, or Sivaguru, or Vararuchi, or the poet-saint Vyasa?' he thought he could trick me into acknowledging one of these identities. But I had written like this! Poor man! He couldn't do anything about it!" Saying this, Bhagavan smiled mischievously at all of us!

Though Bhagavan had disclaimed all superhuman attributes and had stated that he was just 'That Self- knowledge that glows within the heart of every living being,' those who had the opportunity to watch Bhagavan interacting with the various creatures around him felt that Amrithanatha had been quite correct in his perception. All the names that Amrithanatha sought to confer upon Bhagavan seem quite appropriate.

* * *

Bhagavan's compassion was boundless, and it was extended to all creatures. Not only human beings, but animals and birds too, were recipients of Bhagavan's Grace. In fact, it often appeared as though animals had a greater claim upon Bhagavan's love than mere human beings! Monkeys, squirrels, and even tigers, leopards and snakes would come to Bhagavan, and he would treat them with incredible affection and compassion. Bhagavan used to say that depending upon one's Karma, even great souls sometimes assumed the most unexpected forms. He forbade his devotees from driving away even the wildest and most ferocious looking animals. He would say that these animals had as much right to approach him, as any human being. On several occasions, Bhagavan has clearly stated that these creatures had come to him, fully aware of his power to set them free from all their bonds.

Whether the 'visitor' was a dog or a monkey, a cow or a crow, Bhagavan would never refer to the creature as 'It'. Every one of them was treated with the utmost courtesy. If any of the devotees happened to illtreat an animal or to show anything less than perfect courtesy while dealing with an animal, Bhagavan would be displeased. He would reprimand the erring devotee saying, "Why do you do that? You do not see anything beyond the outer form. You have no idea about the soul within. What makes you so sure that you are superior to these creatures? They have also come into the world in the same way as we have. Do they not have the same privileges that we human beings claim for ourselves? Why should you try to drive them away?" Bhagavan protected the dumb creatures that came to him, and showered his love upon them.

From the time when Bhagavan was staying on the Hill, monkeys used to visit him regularly. They would approach Bhagavan with the utmost confidence. They would bring their disputes to him for his judgement! He could understand their language, and could communicate with them easily. On several occasions, Bhagavan heard the monkeys' complaints about each other and settled their disputes to the satisfaction of all the parties involved! The Telugu book, Ramana Leela records numerous incidents involving Bhagavan's interaction with monkeys.

There was one monkey who enjoyed special privileges. While Bhagavan was staying in the Virupaksha Cave, this monkey would saunter in and climb onto Bhagavan's lap. Bhagavan affectionately called him 'Nondi' (the lame one) and would joke with him, saying, "Nondi! If you ever become King, please remember all of us!" Bhagavan's words came true and Nondi really became the King of the monkey clan. One day, he brought his queens and his entire retinue and proudly paraded them before Bhagavan. Bhagavan immediately arranged for a grand feast for the entire monkey clan, to celebrate Nondi's 'coronation'! Bhagavan's extraordinary involvement with the joys and troubles of his monkey friends cannot fail to remind us of the close ties between Lord Rama and the monkey bands led by Sri Hanuman. Indeed, Amrithanatha was quite right in comparing Bhagavan to Sri Hari.

* * *

Then of course, there is Lakshmi! Lakshmi the cow was the undisputed queen of the cowshed. She was like a beloved daughter to Bhagavan. She was an unusually intelligent animal, and seemed to know just how much of a VIP she was! She would walk into the hall unhindered, and serenely go up to Bhagavan's sofa, with all the human devotees hurriedly making way for her royal progress! Lakshmi knew the mealtimes and snacktimes very well indeed. Bhagavan would feed her bananas with his own hands and she would relish the delicacy with her eyes closed in ecstasy. Lakshmi had a special liking for a particular type of banana, (the deliciously sweet variety known as the hill banana). Whenever someone brought these fruits to the Ashram, Bhagavan would say, "This is Lakshmi's favourite. Let us keep it aside for her."

Lakshmi enjoyed all sorts of privileges. It would appear that she knew exactly how much of a favourite she was!

Sometimes, like a pampered child, she would do something naughty, like trampling the kitchen garden. Naturally, such behaviour was not appreciated by the Ashram workers and they would drive the cow away, with harsh words and threatening gestures. But Bhagavan would always come to the cow's defence saying, "It was your fault for not being more careful. You should have erected a fence around the kitchen garden. Why are you scolding poor Laksmi?"

Every Friday, Lakshmi would be dressed up with special care. The attendants would apply turmeric powder on her face and place garlands around her neck and on the tips of her horns. A bright vermilion dot would adorn her forehead. Bedecked like this, Lakshmi would go straight to Bhagavan and stand perfectly still while he caressed her. Sometimes, she would lick Bhagavan's hands, in a special display of affection. Bhagavan's hands would become red with the repeated licks of her rough tongue, but he would patiently submit to her affectionate caresses without complaining.

On *Mattu Pongal* day (the day after the *Sankaranti* festival, when Tamilians worship cows) Lakshmi would always receive special attention. On one such day, Bhagavan's devotees requested him to pose for a photograph with Lakshmi. Bhagavan asked for the cow to be brought to the centre of the cowshed. A space was cleared and Lakshmi came to stand beside Bhagavan, tossing her head like a pretty young girl. Bhagavan stood up from his chair and stood near Lakshmi, stroking her neck and shoulder and murmuring soothingly in her ears. At Bhagavan's touch, Lakshmi quietened down and posed like a seasoned model! Supporting himself with a stick held in his right hand, and with his left arm around Lakshmi's neck, Bhagavan stood there, looking like Sri Krishna Himself. Three or four photos were taken on this occasion. These also seem to support Amrithanatha's comparison of Bhagavan with Hari.

* * *

From the earliest period, that is, from the time when Bhagavan used to live on the Hill, peacocks had always been his companions. A few of these peacocks had set up a unique relationship with Bhagavan. Bhagavan himself has recounted the story of one of his peacock companions. He says, "Even after I came to Skandasramam, Palaniswami continued to stay in the Virupaksha cave. He was quite old by that time and so, it was not possible for him to go up and down the Hill frequently. He stayed in the Virupaksha cave and every evening, I would visit him there just to make sure that he was quite well. Every time I set out for the Virupaksha cave, a peacock would come all the way with me. He would accompany me to the cave and would wait for me for an hour. At the end of one hour, however, he would become quite restless and peck at my feet, take a few steps in the direction of Skandasramam, and check to see whether I was following. If I was still in the cave when he looked back, he would return to the cave and peck at my feet again. He would not leave me alone until I started back, and would walk beside me all the way back to the Skandasramam. Once, Palaniswami was sick and I was reluctant to leave him alone. The peacock was afraid that I might decide to spend the night with Palaniswami. Of course, Palaniswami would have preferred that, but the peacock was determined to take me back to the Skandasramam. The peacock refused to leave my side until I was back in Skandasramam!"

In 1945, the Maharani of Baroda gave Bhagavan a beautiful white peacock. This bird stayed by Bhagavan's side all the time. It enjoyed so much privilege in the Ashram that a cage was set up for it just by the side of Bhagavan's sofa. Bhagavan would talk to this peacock, just as he talked to human beings.

There was one peacock which always waited for Bhagavan's arrival at the entrance to the cowshed, and another one which accompanied him on his walks on the Hill. There has always been a large flock of peacocks in the Ashram and visitors to the Ashram are first welcomed by a reception committee made up of these brightly coloured birds. To see Bhagavan with his shaved head, wearing just a loin-cloth and surrounded by peacocks, was like seeing the Lord of Palani, Sri Subrahmanya Himself! A number of devotees have visualised Bhagavan as Lord Subrahmanya. So, Amrithanatha's comparison of Bhagavan with Lord Subrahmanya is no exaggeration.

* * *

As for the other two terms used by Amrithanatha, namely 'Vararuchi' and 'Yativara', hardly any explanation is required. Bhagavan was a gifted poet. Even Kavyakanta Ganapati Muni acknowledged that Bhagavan's prowess as a poet was far superior to his own. Bhagavan was able to compose a Telugu poem in a verse-form that Kavyakanta was unable to adopt. Furthermore, Bhagavan explained the intricacies of the grammatical rules governing that kind of verse. Bhagavan has explained obscure rules of grammar to great scholars. Bhagavan's knowledge and versatility as a poet are beyond compare. So, equating Bhagavan to Vararuchi is quite apt and totally natural. The term 'Yativara' means 'The greatest of Seers'. Even the Heads of Maths have acknowledged Bhagavan's unique stature. He was truly the greatest of all Seers. Thus we see that Amrithanatha has described Bhagavan accurately, by comparing him to Hari, Siva Guru, Vararuchi and Yativara.

6. Sri Ramana Sannidhimurai

Sri Ramana Sannidhimurai is a work of unparalleled beauty and immeasurable depth of meaning. *Sannidhimurai* is a Tamil word meaning "listing out one's grievances in the Presence of God." In other words, it is a form of poetry in which the devotee prays to the Almighty and begs for His indulgence. The same phrase can also be translated as 'a set of rules for the conduct of worship in the Divine Presence.'

The author of this work is Sri Muruganar, a highly learned Tamil scholar of eminence and a poet. More importantly, Muruganar was an ardent devotee of Bhagavan Sri Ramana Maharshi. His was an absolute and unconditional surrender at the feet of Bhagavan. So much so that he could not even think of any other deity. Sri Ramana Sannidhimurai is in praise of Bhagavan. It captivated the hearts of Bhagavan's devotees to such an extent that they used to memorise long passages from the book and recite them in Bhagavan's presence.

In the olden days, *Saivite* saints used to compose hymns on the presiding deities of every temple they visited. All these hymns were gathered together and compiled into what came to be called the Panniru Tirumurai, (Panniru means twelve in Tamil). These hymns are all inspired poetry of the highest order. The sweetness of language and the beauty of expression are such that these songs have survived all these years, inspiring generation after generation of Lord Siva's devotees.

Apart from the *Panniru Tirumurai*, there are a number of individual *Sannidhimurais*, sung by various poets through the ages. Even in modern times, the practice of composing *Sannidhimurai* continues. The *Tirupporur Sannidhimurai* was composed by Sri Chidambara Swami in recent times. When

Muruganar composed *Sri Ramana Sannidhimurai*, he was only continuing a well-established tradition. *Sri Ramana Sannidhimurai*, however, has some unique characteristics which set it apart from all other *Sannidhimurais*. The songs in the *Panniru Tirumurai* were sung by several different poets, at several different temples, over a long period of time. The *Ramana Sannidhimurai* (except for the 12th chapter) is the work of a single poet, with all the poems extolling the praises of a single Deity. Moreover, Sri Muruganar has included some songs in verse-forms that are not found in the *Panniru Tirumurai*. The crowning glory of the *Ramana Sannidhimurai* is the chapter describing the extraordinary power of Bhagavan's "Glance of Grace" (*Kannokkam*). Bhagavan had the power to transport a devotee to a higher plane through a mere glance of his eyes. Sri Muruganar tells us that a single glance from Bhagavan's eyes can grant Liberation to a devotee, and free him from the cycle of birth and death.

The story of how the *Ramana Sannidhimurai* came to be written is very interesting. Even before his first visit to Tirvannamalai, Sri Muruganar had developed a very high regard for Bhagavan, hearing about him from his devotees and from reading Bhagavan's works. Every time he read the *Tiruvachakam* (a devotional song composed by the poet-saint Manickavachakar), Muruganar would be filled with the longing that, just as Manickavachakar had found a suitable Guru, he too should have the good fortune to find a Guru soon. It was in this state of mind that Muruganar came to Tiruvannamalai.

On reaching Tiruvannamalai, Muruganar went to the Arunachaleswara Temple to thank God for making his trip to Tiruvannamalai possible. While in the temple, he felt that he should take some suitable offering for Bhagavan. So he sat down

in the temple hall and composed a decad of verses and took it
with him to Ramanasramam. These are the ten verses known as
the *Desika Padikam*. (In Tamil and Sanskrit, the word *Desika*
means Guru).

Upon entering the Ashram, Muruganar was assailed by
doubts. He felt that he was ignorant about the etiquette to be
followed when meeting a great sage. As Muruganar stood
hesitating at the entrance to the hall, Bhagavan himself came
out of the hall and came towards the spot where Muruganar
was standing. It was as if the Guru had come to welcome his
disciple!

The sight of Bhagavan took Muruganar's breath away.
For a few minutes, he just stood there, drinking in Bhagavan's
form with his eyes. Suddenly, he remembered the verses he had
written. He took out the piece of paper and tried to read from
it. But his eyes were flooded with tears and his voice was choked
with emotion. He was incapable of reading anything. In the
end, Bhagavan himself had to take the paper from Muruganar's
hands and read the verses himself. So great was Bhagavan's
compassion for his devotee that he took the trouble to read all
the ten verses, standing at the entrance of the hall, while the
author of those verses just stood and gazed at him!

Afterwards Muruganar would write poems once in a while
and lay them at Bhagavan's feet. Upon reading one of these poems,
Bhagavan significantly remarked with grace, "These lines are just
like the verses in Manickavachakar's *Tiruvachakam*. Why don't
you write some more verses like these? If you continue to compose
verses in the same way, you can write another *Tiruvachakam!*"
Hearing these words, Muruganar was overcome by emotion. He
was so moved by Bhagavan's confidence in him that he broke
down. Through his sobs he stammered, "Bhagavan, in your

compassion, you have compared me to the great poet-saint. It is true that you are the Lord Siva Himself. But I am a worthless creature. I am not worthy of being compared to Manickavachakar. Where is the shining star and where is the firefly? I am not capable of emulating Manickavachakar on whom divine grace had descended in abundance."

Bhagavan listened to Muruganar but did not answer in words. His only response was a long deep look into Muruganar's eyes. This one glance was powerful enough to inspire in him the confidence to start writing poetry of rare beauty. He started composing verses regularly. Coming to know of this, a devotee, N.R.Krishnamoorthy Iyer said to him, "These poems are quite good and it would be good idea to systematically compile them into a *Sannidhimurai*." Thus the *Ramana Sannidhimurai* started taking shape. Muruganar firmly believed that Bhagavan made use of him as an instrument for the creation of this work. Several stanzas in *Ramana Sannidhimurai* bring out this idea.

Bhagavan's glance of grace had the power to uplift a person and impart spiritual knowledge. Through more than thirty verses titled *Thiruk Kannokkam* (Divine Glance), Muruganar describes the power of Bhagavan's Glance of Grace, and ends each verse with a plea for the bestowal of this Glance on the devotees.

7. COMPOSITION OF RAMANA PURANAM

Ramana Sannidhimurai of Muruganar has been modelled on the *Tiruvachakam* of Manickavachakar. The very first chapter in *Tiruvachakam* is a very beautiful one, titled *Siva Puranam*. But the first edition of the *Ramana Sannidhimurai* did not contain an equivalent chapter. Muruganar wanted to correct this inadequacy, and so he started composing the same chapter.

He had written some lines, when he was suddenly assailed by doubts regarding the appropriate title for this particular chapter.

As Muruganar had followed the model of *Tiruvachakam*, he should have given the same title for this chapter also. But he wanted to name it *Ramana Puranam* instead of *Siva Puranam* to signify that these songs were in praise of the living God, Sri Ramana. He also felt obliged to follow the original in every detail. Unable to come to a decision, Muruganar gathered up the papers of this unfinished chapter and laid the bundle at Bhagavan's feet. He did not say anything to Bhagavan about the confusion in his mind and left the hall. It was evening by the time he returned to the hall again. As soon as Muruganar entered the hall, Bhagavan beckoned him close, gave him back the bundle of papers and said, "Have a look at the papers." Immediately, Muruganar opened the bundle and started reading.

One glance was enough! Muruganar was speechless with surprise. He had not mentioned his confusion to Bhagavan; neither had he asked for Bhagavan's advice. But the Master had answered the disciple's unspoken question in the most unmistakable manner. At the top of the page was the title *Ramana Puranam*. Not only that, Bhagavan had written *Ramana Puranam* on top of every single page! And moreover, he had added many more lines of poetry to Muruganar's own composition.*

When the second edition of *Ramana Sannidhimurai* was prepared for publication, Muruganar added the *Ramana Puranam*. While checking the proofs, Muruganar made a mark in the text and added a footnote saying that only a portion of this chapter had been his own work and that the rest of the lines beyond the mark had been composed by Sri Bhagavan himself.

---

* The present edition of *Ramana Sannidhimurai* contains 540 lines of *Ramana Puranam*.

After correcting the proofs, Muruganar handed over the copy to Bhagavan and requested him to check it. Bhagavan noticed the mark Muruganar had made, and read the footnote. At once, he turned to Muruganar and said, "So! Only this portion is Bhagavan's, is it?" These words had shattering effect on Muruganar. He fell at Bhagavan's feet and sobbed, "Bhagavan! What a grave mistake I have made! Please forgive me. I have not done anything at all. It is all your work. Every single line of poetry owes its existence to your infinite grace." The mark and the footnote were removed immediately. This incident is sufficient proof that the *Ramana Sannidhimurai* was composed only by the grace of Bhagavan Sri Ramana.

* * *

Upadesa Undhiar adorns the central portion of *Ramana Sannidhimurai*. The *Bhagavad Gita*, which is the essence of Sri Krishna's teachings, is at the heart of the *Mahabharata*. Similarly, the *Upadesa Undhiar* (which was later translated into Sanskrit, Telugu and Malayalam by Bhagavan as *Upadesa Saram*), the essence of Bhagavan's teachings, forms the central portion of *Ramana Sannidhimurai*. In this beautiful song, Bhagavan has condensed the lessons taught by all the *Upanishads* and set them down in one comprehensive poem. Incidentally *Upadesa Undhiar* is the only work composed in the form of a book by Bhagavan.

Ramana Sannidhimurai has yet another distinction. Bhagavan has stated that it is equal to *Tiruvachakam* in all respects. Bhagavan has given his endorsement in the form of a poem.

* * *

Visvanatha Swami, one of Bhagavan's disciples, was also an intimate friend of Muruganar. Muruganar had a passionate love for the Tamil language. This made him change his original name of 'Ramanathapuram Subrahmanyam' to 'Mugavapuri Murugan'. (Mugavapuri is the Tamil name for his birthplace — Ramanathapuram and 'Murugan' is the Tamil equivalent of his name — Subrahmanyam). Visvanatha Swami was amused by Muruganar's fastidiousness and liked to tease him. Once, while he was in the hall with Bhagavan and a few other devotees, Visvanatha Swami kept repeating the phrase, 'Mugavapuri Murugan'. Bhagavan noticed this and said to him, "Visvanatha! Instead of simply chanting it, why don't you compose a poem using those two words?" Visvanatha Swami immediately took out a piece of paper and very enthusiastically began his poem with the words 'Mugavapuri Murugan'. Try as he might, however, he could not think of anything beyond these two words. At last, in sheer frustration, he went out, leaving the paper with Bhagavan. By the time Visvanatha Swami returned, Bhagavan had a lovely poem ready. Apart from the two words, 'Mugavapuri Murugan', nothing had been written by Visvanatha Swami. Nevertheless, Bhagavan had signed the poem, 'Visvanathan', thus attributing its composition to Visvanatha Swami. A translation of the poem follows:

"Arunachala Ramana, the One who resides in the lotus of my heart, laughed at my foolish ego and destroyed it completely with a single glance. He then proceeded to shower His Grace upon me, Mugavapuri Murugan, to enable me to enlighten the entire world with the *Murai* (*Ramana Sannidhimurai*), which is comparable to the *Tiruvachakam*."

Muruganar has composed more than 30,000 poems in sweet, pure Tamil and most of these works like *Guruvachaka Kovai*, *Ramana Anubhoothi*, and *Sri Ramana Jnana Bhodham* (in 9 volumes) have already appeared in book form.

8. RAMAKRISHNA IYER

My uncle Ramakrishna Iyer, was one of the earlier devotees to come to Bhagavan. He had surrendered himself to Bhagavan while the Master was staying in the Virupaksha Cave. Ramakrishna Iyer's younger brother, Ranganatha Iyer, is my father. Our ancestral village is Padi Agraharam, in Chengam Taluk. This village is about 20 miles to the west of Tiruvannamalai. This is where my uncle and my father were born. In their adult years, both the brothers settled down in Tiruvannamalai. My uncle was the Munsif of Tiruvannamalai Town. This being an influential position, my uncle's family was comfortably placed in life. My father was a contractor. His work took him to the Kurnool District of Andhra Pradesh, and he eventually settled down there. But even after establishing his business in Andhra Pradesh, my father could never stay away from Tiruvannamalai for long. He often visited his brother, and would go with him to Ramanasramam. It is only because of my elders' devotion to Bhagavan that I came into his fold eventually.

In addition to his work in Tiruvannamalai, my uncle also had the job of contractor in the salt-pans of Pondicherry. He was a man of very generous nature. He made liberal donations to Ramanasramam, and assisted the Ashram authorities in all their activities. Chinnaswami had a special regard for my uncle. Whenever important visitors came to the Ashram, my uncle would be informed immediately.

My uncle's wife, Ponnammal was an extraordinary lady. She had no worldly attachments at all. She had received initiation from Kavyakanta Ganapati Muni, and was constantly engaged in prayers and puja. She paid little attention to household affairs. Nevertheless, the household functioned quite smoothly, and there was no dearth of visitors to the house.

My aunt was a beautiful lady with a radiant face. She never plaited her hair, but let it hang loose all the time. She worshipped Goddess Shakti. She used to say that because of her intense devotion to the Goddess, she experienced something like an electric shock, if ever her bare feet touched the ground. So, she always wore a pair of wooden sandals on her feet. She never wore any jewels on her person.

If relatives or guests arrived unexpectedly, my aunt would immediately pick up her slippers and go into her room. She neither welcomed visitors nor objected to their visits. She simply did not get involved in taking care of guests. But my uncle never complained about this. Instead, he took care of the details himself. There was a young Brahmin boy to take care of the cooking and my uncle managed all the other household affairs.

In any situation, the Ashram authorities could depend upon my uncle for prompt and generous assistance. Once, Chinnaswami sent word that the priest who usually performed the puja at the Ashram temple had not come that day. Immediately, my uncle sent his cook to the Ashram, so that the puja could be performed on time. In the early days, the Ashram had to deal with a number of problems. Every time trouble arose, my uncle used to take charge of the situation and try to find a suitable solution for the problem. When thieves broke into the Ashram it was my uncle whom Kunjuswami fetched from the Town. My uncle could always be depended upon, to assist the Ashram authorities in every possible manner. Whenever the need arose, Chinnaswami would send word to him, and my uncle never let him down.

My aunt had a great regard for Kavyakanta Ganapati Muni (Nayana). Very often, Nayana would come to stay in my uncle's house, with a group of his disciples. All their needs were well taken care of. Even after Nayana set up his own house in Tiruvannamalai, my aunt used to send provisions and other essentials to his house, through the servants. My uncle never objected to this practice.

In the same way, my aunt did not object to the streams of visitors who arrived at the house, especially during the Deepam and other Temple festivals. All the guests were assured of a very comfortable stay, and my aunt never interfered with my uncle's arrangements for their welfare. My uncle and aunt had an excellent understanding and a high regard for each other. Neither of them ever criticised or even questioned the activities of the other. They were an unusual couple. Though they lived within the framework of family life, they had no worldly attachments.

This unique couple had only one son named Radhakrishnan and everybody called him 'Radha'. He had acquired his parents' unique qualities. Worldly pursuits held no attraction for him. He was devoted to Bhagavan, and spent all his spare time in Ramanasramam. Bhagavan had a special regard for this young man. Radha spent all his college vacations in the Ashram. He would often go around the Hill with Bhagavan. He spent all his time in spiritual pursuits, under the guidance of Bhagavan.

Neither Radha nor his mother showed any interest or involvement in the affairs of the relatives. My uncle alone attended weddings and other family functions. The poorer relatives could always count upon my uncle for generous monetary help in all situations.

Radha finished his studies and found employment as an engineer in the Railways.

He requested his parents to come and live with him. But my uncle refused to leave Tiruvannamalai and Bhagavan. In the end, Radha was forced to leave my uncle to manage on his own. He took his mother with him and looked after her with great affection and dedication.

After a while, my uncle started having some difficulty in living alone. He stayed with us in Madras for some time. He also stayed at Ramanasramam for a while. Occasionally, he would go to stay with his son for a few days. In his last days, my uncle was in Ramanasramam, where Chinnaswami took very good care of him. But in spite of the best treatment, my uncle's health declined rapidly. Finally, the Ashram authorities sent word to Radha. He came immediately and took his father to his house, and did his best to restore his father's failing health. But all of Radha's efforts were in vain. In 1934, my uncle Ramakrishna Iyer breathed his last.

9. Do not touch those Seeds!

From a very young age, my uncle's son Radha showed interest in spiritual matters. In his childhood, Radha used to accompany his father to Ramanasramam almost every day. He developed a great love for Bhagavan, and Bhagavan was especially gracious to the little boy. During the Skandasramam period, Radha would rush up the Hill every evening after school. He brought a flask of coffee with him, and would invariably reach the Skandasramam by 5o'clock. He would return home only after dark. He used to converse freely with Bhagavan, and would insist upon staying close to Bhagavan all the time.

After he finished school, Radha went to Madras and joined the Christian College. During those years, he kept up a regular correspondence with Bhagavan. All his holidays were spent at

Ramanasramam with Bhagavan. Just before leaving Madras, Radha would write to Bhagavan and tell him that he would be arriving at the Ashram soon and express his desire to go around the Hill with him! Once, when Appu Sastri a devotee, asked Bhagavan whether they could go for Giripradakshinam, Bhagavan replied, "Radha has written to say that he will be arriving here tomorrow. He will certainly insist upon going around the Hill with me. Let us wait for him, and do the Giripradakshinam tomorrow."

On these long walks around the Arunachala Hill, Bhagavan would support himself with an arm around Radha's shoulders. Once, just before setting out on *giripradakshina*, the devotees thought up a plan of taking up one subject each for discussion in turn. According to the rules of the game, each person had to give a short speech on some topic of their choice. Everybody made an effort, but Radha kept quiet. Kunjuswami noticed this and said, "Come on, Radha! It is your turn now. What are you going to talk about?" In reply, Radha said, "Do *jivanmuktas* (liberated souls) have to speak? Do they ever make speeches?" On hearing this, Bhagavan smiled and said, "Oh! Don't *jivanmuktas* speak, then?" All the others were amazed by Radha's rather unusual response, but Bhagavan seemed to be very pleased.

Something very interesting happened, on another occasion. Radha had come to the Ashram. Bhagavan was just leaving for Palakothu. As Bhagavan always walked barefoot, and as the stones on the path were often burning hot, the devotees had decided to plant some shade-giving trees along the path. They had dug a row of pits along the path and had some seeds ready for planting. They wanted Bhagavan to plant the seeds with his hands and so they were waiting for him to come there. They had the seeds on a tray.

When Bhagavan came to the spot, he saw the pits and the group of devotees gathered there. He asked, "What is going on?" The devotees explained their plans and requested Bhagavan to plant the seeds with his own hands. Just as Bhagavan reached out to pick up a seed from the tray, there was a loud shout from Radha. Everybody was startled to see Radha running towards them, shouting, "Bhagavan! Bhagavan! Please don't touch those seeds!" Bhagavan exclaimed, "What is this? All of you told me to sow these seeds. Now Radha is telling me not to touch them. What am I to do?" Everyone turned to Radha, waiting for an explanation for his behavior. By this time, Radha was in tears. In between sobs, he stammered, "Bhagavan! Do you know what these people are planning to do? They want to grow shade-giving trees along the path. But if you touch those seeds, the whole purpose of the exercise would be defeated! One look from your eyes is enough to set a man free from the cycle of birth and death. When this is so, what will happen to those seeds if your hands touch them? Will they not attain liberation immediately? How, then, can they grow into trees?"

Everyone was stunned by Radha's explanation for his strange behaviour. Bhagavan gave him a keen look, but did not say anything. Actually, Radha's fears were well founded. Just a few months previous to this incident, Radha, Kunjuswami and Bhagavan had planted some onion seeds in the kitchen garden. As they were planting the seeds, they were jocularly remarking among themselves that they would watch out as to whose seeds would grow into the sturdiest plants. A few days later, Kunjuswami's and Radha's seeds had become healthy little plants, but none of the seeds planted by Bhagavan had germinated. Radha told the devotees about this incident, and explained the reason for his apparently strange behaviour. The devotees were thrilled and moved when they heard this story from Radha. Bhagavan, too, appeared to be pleased by Radha's perceptive observations.

All through his life, he lived like an ascetic, attending to his duties without any attachment or emotional involvement. He lived according to Bhagavan's precepts, constantly practising Self- enquiry and meditating upon Bhagavan's teachings. In 1950, the same year as Bhagavan's Nirvana, Radha shed his mortal body and attained the lotus feet of his Master.

10. My longing to stay at Sri Ramanasramam

Every time my parents took me to my uncle's house, my uncle Ramakrishna Iyer would arrange for us all to visit Ramanasramam to see Bhagavan. On one occasion, my uncle had some work to do, and could not take me to the Ashram himself. So he sent me with one of our relatives.

I was around 8 years old at the time. Somehow, this particular visit has stayed fresh in my memory all these years. When we reached the Ashram, we found Bhagavan sitting on a small platform at the entrance to a thatched shed. I prostrated myself before Bhagavan and then stood watching him silently. Bhagavan enquired something of my companion and he replied to him. I do not remember the conversation now. But I remember the beatific smile Bhagavan gave me. The memory of that smile has stayed with me ever afterwards. On every subsequent visit to the Ashram, I would think of that enchanting smile!

While I was in the fifth standard, I had a lesson on Sri Ramakrishna Paramahamsa. That lesson made a profound impression on my mind. I felt inspired by Sri Ramakrishna's story, and it awakened in me a desire for a life free from all worldly attachments. I wanted to dedicate myself to spiritual pursuits and it grew stonger with the passage of time.

As if to strengthen my resolve, a couple of incidents occurred soon afterwards. The first incident was the death of a neighbour. When I saw his wife's grief, I thought, "She is in this situation only because she got married. Marriage must, therefore, be considered the main cause of her misery."

The same evening, there was some festival in the temple and the deity was taken out in a grand procession as a part of the ongoing festival. As the procession passed in front of our house, I saw a *devadasi* dancing at the head of the procession. The two images, one of the grieving widow I had seen in the morning, and the other of the dancing girl, flashed into my mind one after the other. I felt convinced that marriage had caused the first woman's misery and that the second woman was able to lead a life of freedom only because she was not married. Then and there, I resolved not to get married.

However, God had willed otherwise. When I was twelve years old, my parents started making arrangements for my marriage. I tried my best to convince my father that marriage was not for me. I begged and pleaded, but my efforts were all in vain. The elders in the family forced my father to finalise my marriage immediately, in spite of my vehement protests.

I felt very badly frustrated and totally helpless. Then one day, I went to my father and expressed my feelings to him in clear terms. I said, "In spite of my repeated protests you have finalised my marriage. I might be young, but my determination is very strong. I am absolutely certain that I cannot lead the life of a married woman. By ignoring my protests, and going ahead with your plans for my marriage, you are making a mistake which you will definitely regret later. If later on, you happen to find yourself in an embarrassing situation, please do not blame me." Now when I think about it, I am amazed at my own boldness. I had never spoken to my father like that before. I think some power beyond my comprehension must have activated me, and given me the courage to talk to my father so boldly at the age of twelve.

My father had a lot of affection for me, and he also had a genuine concern for my feelings. But he was quite helpless. It must have been extremely difficult for him to take a decision; I appreciate that now! At the time, my father said, "Kanaka, all the arrangements for your marriage have already been finalised. So, please co-operate with us now. Later on, if you continue to feel as you do now, I will try to comply with your wishes. I will not try to force you into anything against your wish. But please do not stop the marriage now, at this stage."

I felt that if this was to be my destiny, I just had to go along. So, I went through the ceremony of marriage without any further protest. When the time came for me to start family-life, however, I brought my resolve into action. Nothing could shake my resolve. The entire household was plunged into gloom. My mother was heartbroken. My father was bound by his promise to me, and did not try to force me to do anything against my wish.

I remained oblivious to all the conflicting emotions of my family members. I calmly continued with my normal routine. I would get up at 3o'clock every morning. After having my bath, I would sit in meditation, under a tree in our garden. After a few hours of quiet meditation, I would engage myself in the performance of puja, recitation of prayers, and reading from the scriptures.

Each time I went to Ramanasramam and saw Bhagavan, my heart would melt and tears would pour down my face. There was a great longing in my heart — a longing to settle down at Ramanasramam. On one of my visits to the Ashram, Bhagavan looked at me and asked, "Where is Radha now?" (Bhagavan was referring to my cousin, Radhakrishnan.) Bhagavan's very first words to me were about Radha! To Bhagavan's question, I replied, "He is now in Guntakal." Bhagavan said, "Oh! So he has left Gudur and gone to Guntakal, has he?" and smiled at me.

In 1944 I visited the Ashram. When I entered the hall and saw the devotees sitting in meditation in his presence, my heart cried silently, "Bhagavan! I long to stay in your presence, just like all these fortunate people. Will my prayers ever be answered? How much longer should I waste my time in journeying to and fro?" The thought brought tears to my eyes. With brimming eyes, I prostrated and stood up. Bhagavan gave me a long look of compassion which moved me. But I was unable to express my anguish in words. I usually remained silent in his presence. Somehow, I could never talk to him openly, even to tell him about the great longing in my heart. His mere *darshan* used to make me inactive.

Many times I had seen devotees approaching Bhagavan with some query or the other, and I had heard Bhagavan clearing their doubts. At times I would think, "I must also ask him something." But immediately a voice within me would say, "Do you really need to tell Bhagavan what is in your heart? Is he not capable of reading your thoughts?" With this thought the desire to ask questions would disappear from my mind. As soon as the desire died out, my mind would become light and free. I could feel a great peace settling on me. All desires for speech and action would disappear and my mind would lay itself down at

Bhagavan's feet completely calm and content. I cannot explain this strange phenomenon. It was not that I feared that Bhagavan might not reply if I asked him something. He was ever gracious to all his devotees, regardless of their individual merits or level of scholarship. I am not capable of describing my own state of mind. Anyway, this feeling did not really bother me much. It did not seem particularly important to me. I just accepted the state of affairs, and never wasted my time trying to find an explanation for it.

My restlessness affected my parents deeply, but their concern for me made it difficult for them to agree to my settling down at Ramanasramam. It took me quite some time to persuade my parents.

A few days before I finally came to Arunachala, I had a strange and wonderful experience. It was very early in the morning, and I was still asleep. It was my normal practice to get up at 4 in the morning and to spend the quiet early morning hours in meditation. On this particular morning, I had not risen from my bed when I felt Bhagavan's presence close to me. I felt that he was sitting beside me, carassing me from the neck to the heart. He smiled at me and said, "What is it that you gave me? Why is it that I love you so much?" As he spoke, he continued to stroke my neck and throat with an infinitely tender touch. I cannot say how long this experience lasted. I am sure it was not just a dream. All my senses were aware of Bhagavan's presence by my side. With his words and his touch, Bhagavan brought a sense of peace and contentment to my restless heart. I have no idea of how long I lay like that. When my sister-in-law noticed that I had not risen at my usual time, she came and woke me up. Even after getting up, I continued to be aware of some unusual feeling deep in my heart. A deep peace had taken possession of my senses. Though I carried on with my routine activities, I was in a dazed state. My parents noticed the change in me. They were finally convinced that family life was not for me. They had no choice but to let me have my way. So, in 1946, I came to Tiruvannamalai, with my parents' permission to stay there permanently. My spiritual journey had begun at last!

11. MY PERMANENT STAY IN TIRUVANNAMALAI

When I came to Tiruvannamalai with the intention of making it my home, there were very few houses in Ramana Nagar. To the west of the Ashram there was the Bose Compound known as 'Mahasthan', with eight houses in it. These houses were occupied mostly by people from the North. Close to the Bose Compound were the Mc.Iver Bungalow and the Dr.T.N.K. Building. A little to the interior, there were a few more houses. These were Ceylon Ramachandra's House, Shanthammal's house with a bungalow just behind it, Kalyanaraman's house and Subrahmanyam's house. These houses were not close to each other but separated from one another by fairly long distances. In the street opposite to the Dakshinamoorthy Temple, there were the houses of Anandammal and Sunita Chatterjee, and also the Sub- Registrar's Compound. On the other side of the street were Komutti Lakshmi Ammal's house and Alamelu Ammal's house.

On the main road, there was the Morvi Guest House which is Ramanasramam's own guest house reserved mainly for visitors belonging to princely families. This is why the Morvi Guest House came to be known as the Royal Building. Beyond this was the Pollachi Goundar Compound with Dr.Syed's Bungalow and Dr. Anantha Narayana Rao's Bungalow close to it. On the other side were Ramanatha Iyer's house and the houses owned by Rajagopala Iyer, Gowri Ammal, Cohen and Taleyarkhan. Behind these buildings, there were Lokammal's house, and Raju Chettiar's Bungalow a little closer to the road. These were the only houses in Ramana Nagar, in those days.

Most of these houses were occupied by the owners themselves and except for one or two buildings none of them had any rooms for rent. Moreover, very few of the houses had electricity and running water. Even the roads were little more than dirt tracks. In the rainy season, the lane leading to Sub-Registrar Narayana Iyer's house would get flooded with rain water and it would become impossible to wade through the ankle-deep water because the sides of the street were full of thorns and stones, and tall ant-hills where snakes had made their homes. There were plenty of water snakes too.

In the beginning, before I found accommodation in Ramana Nagar, I stayed with some relatives in Tiruvannamalai Town. Every morning, I would quickly finish my ablutions and hurry to the Ashram. I would get there in time for the *Upanishad* recitations which started at 5 a.m. everyday. Breakfast and lunch were at the Ashram. After lunch I would go to some devotee's house and rest for a while. By 3 o'clock I would be back in the Ashram. At 5 in the evening, there would be chanting of the Vedas. I would listen to this before returning to the town along with other devotees. In those days, there was no arrangement for ladies to stay in the Ashram, during the night.

It was not easy to go to the Ashram from the town every morning. The distance was not the only problem. The Government Hospital on Chengam Road marked the limit of Tiruvannamalai Town. Beyond this, there were no houses or buildings of any kind. It was just a long, deserted stretch of road, with some dense woods here and there along the way. It was definitely not safe for a young woman to walk along this road alone early in the morning. I did not like to trouble my hosts by asking for someone to accompany me to the Ashram every morning. But I could not make the trip alone either. Somehow, 15 days passed without any solution being found. But I knew that this state of affairs could not continue much longer. I started looking for some accommodation closer to the Ashram. My relative and I made enquiries and searched for a suitable place for me to stay. At last, we were able to secure a room in Komutti Lakshmi Ammal's house.

There were six portions in the compound. My room was at the extreme end of the building. Beyond my room, there was some open space which served as a dumping ground for all kinds of rubbish. Along the fence at the back, there were several ant-hills which made it abundantly clear that I would have snakes for company. The room itself was very small, nothing more than four mud walls and a thatched roof. There was a large gap between the top of the door and the roof. This made it easy for cats and rats to visit me regularly! There was no electricity, and no running water. There was a well in the compound, but the water in it was very muddy. The first person to use the well in the morning would be lucky enough to get fairly clear water, but everyone who came later would have to make do with muddy water. Even this was limited in quantity. One could somehow manage to have a quick bath, but washing clothes was out of the question.

In spite of all these disadvantages, I considered myself lucky to have found a room so close to the Ashram. I bought some pots and pans from a shop near the temple, and arranged my things in my new home. Gradually, I settled into some kind of a routine. Every two or three days, a few of us would go to the Munsif's house and wash our clothes in the well there. This had to be done between 12 noon and 2 pm only, as I had to be back at the Ashram at 3 pm. Drying the washed clothes posed another problem. I could not leave my clothes hanging outside my room. My room being at the back of the building, and with the absence of a compound wall, there was a good chance of my clothes getting stolen while I was away. So, I used to gather up the half-dried clothes and put them inside my room before leaving for the Ashram.

In those days, for cooking I did not have a gas stove or a kerosene stove. I had to manage with coal and wood. Moreover, I had very little time for cooking. After the early morning Upanishad recitation, I would come home at 6.15 or so, and I had to return to the Ashram by 8 o'clock. I had to finish my cooking within that short gap. Most of the time, I made only rice and just a single side-dish — sometimes *rasam*, sometimes some *chutney*. Even this would seem too much trouble sometimes, and I would make do with curds and pickles. On the rare occasions when I could manage to cook some vegetables, the curry or sambhar seemed like some exotic delicacy! Even the most frugal meal had to be stored very carefully. Big field rats often entered my room during my absence, and they would upset all the vessels and scatter the contents all over the floor. To prevent this, I used to invert a big drum over the food-containers, and place a large stone on top of the drum.

I came to the Ashram in 1946. The War was going on then, and rationing was in force. Rice, sugar, kerosene — everything was in short supply. In fact, there was not enough petrol for the buses and charcoal was used to run them!

The reader might feel that, at that time, my life was full of problems, and that I must have been quite miserable. But it was not like that at all! I never felt the burden of my problems, because the sight of Bhagavan's face early in the morning was enough to drive out all worries from my mind, and fill it with joy and peace. A single smile could set my heart soaring. I would feel proud of myself for having been singled out for such a rare privilege! It is impossible to describe the charm of Bhagavan's smile. It has to be experienced personally! It is hard to believe that so much power was packed into that frail frame. Bhagavan was very simple in his appearance, and he engaged himself in the most ordinary activities. Yet, one had but to look at that charming figure reclining upon the sofa, to become totally captivated!

In spite of all the difficulties and the frustrations of my domestic life, every morning my heart sang at the very thought of spending one more day in his presence, gazing at that enchanting form, and listening to his electrifying words. Even as I entered the Ashram, I could feel a transformation within myself. All my petty worries disappeared as if by magic. I felt as if each one of my faculties was slowly calming down. At the first glimpse of Bhagavan's form, my ego would start disintegrating. As I drew nearer and nearer to him I became more and more like an empty shell, a body without a mind. It is difficult to describe this feeling. At times, it was as though I was totally detached from my body. It took an effort of will to drag my body along. I was in a state of ecstasy which made it impossible for me to function in the normal way.

Sometimes, as I approached the hall, I would realise that Bhagavan had directed his eyes at me. His look rendered me powerless. It destroyed my ego and left me feeling light and peaceful. The intensity of his gaze was, at times, almost impossible to bear. It made me feel that walking up to Bhagavan's sofa was a task beyond my capability. On such occasions, I would settle down just near the entrance. My mind would get completely absorbed in the Self, without any kind of effort on my part. Bhagavan has granted me this blissful expreience on many occasions. For a long time after leaving the hall, the peace and the joy of the experience lingered on.

Though Bhagavan's glance alone was powerful enough to satisfy all my spiritual needs, at times I couldn't help feeling the desire to ask him some question and to listen to his answer. I would never dare to approach Bhagavan, while others were nearby. But sometimes, it would so happen that the hall was almost empty when I arrived at the Ashram. On those occasions, I would gather up all my courage and approach Bhagavan's sofa, with the intention of asking him something. But as I neared the sofa, he would direct his gaze upon me. My mind disappeared without trace. I lost all desire for speech. Certainly this was a manifestation of his grace. Once I had reached this state, it was, of course, impossible for me to sustain the desire to ask anything. But though I could never manage to ask any questions directly, I eagerly absorbed Bhagavan's answers to other people's questions. Bhagavan's words contained the rarest philosophical truths, and my mind kept savouring them for a long time afterwards.

Many of Bhagavan's devotees conversed with him very freely. While engaged in conversation, Bhagavan's graceful gestures and his laughing eyes were captivating. Bhagavan never acknowledged anyone as his disciple. Neither did he give religious discourses. His life itself was his teaching. Even seemingly casual remarks were full of meaning and an earnest seeker could find a valuable lesson in every look, word and gesture.

12. INITIATION THROUGH LOOK

The consecration of the Matrubhuteswara Temple took place on the 17th of March, 1949. At the entrance of the temple, there is a large hall. At one end of this hall, a throne-like sofa was installed and Bhagavan was requested to sit upon it. Bhagavan's sofa was carved out of a single block of black stone. We usually classify anything hard as being 'like a stone'. But this particular stone must have been extraordinarily pliable! It has allowed itself to be carved into an object of exquisite beauty. The most intricate designs have been carved into this stone throne. Surely, this is only due to Bhagavan's Grace. He who could melt the hardest heart with his compassion, must have softened this stone also!

For a while, Bhagavan used to recline upon this stone sofa. On either side of the sofa, there was space for the devotees to sit down and meditate. Male devotees would sit on the Eastern side of the hall and the ladies would be seated on the Western side. Devotees filled the space in front of the sofa as well. This arrangement made it possible for the devotees to feast their eyes upon Bhagavan's enchanting form, from both sides and from the front as well. Wherever one might be seated, however, Bhagavan's compassionate gaze would fall upon every single person. I usually sat close to the window, on the southern side of the hall, facing Bhagavan. Rani Majumdar, a Bengali lady from the Bose Compound, would sit beside me. One day, for some reason, there was nobody in the front row. Rani Majumdar said, "See, there is nobody in the front row. Let us go and sit there today." This was a tempting idea indeed! Seeing the two of us moving to a space so close to Bhagavan, Kameswaramma, (another lady devotee) also came to sit beside us.

I prostrated myself before Bhagavan and settled down. From that instant, Bhagavan's eyes stayed on me. If you want to look at Bhagavan, you must choose a time when he isn't looking directly at you! When his gaze is upon you, something happens, which makes it impossible for you to keep your eyes open. The intensity of Bhagavan's direct look is too much for an ordinary human being to take. It is as though some invisible power has entered you and made its way to the very core of your being and there is nothing but the blissful awareness of the Self.

For a short while, I gazed at Bhagavan with my eyes open. Within a few seconds, my eyes closed of their own accord, and I was totally immersed in a peace that is beyond description. I do not know how long I stayed in that state of bliss. After a while, I managed to open my eyes. I saw that Bhagavan's gaze was still upon me. He had not changed his position; nor had he lifted that magical look from me. I closed my eyes again.

After a while, I heard voices and opened my eyes to see what was happening. Srinivasa Rao (Mouni) had come in with the day's mail. Bhagavan was going through the letters and other correspondence. After sometime, Mouni left the hall. Bhagavan too got up and went out towards the cowshed, accompanied by his personal attendant. At that point of time, I stood up and went back to my usual place under the window.

Kameswaramma followed me. She was in a very emotional state. She embraced me and, with tears in her eyes said, "Kanakamma! You are indeed very fortunate. What a wonderful experience you have had! From the time you sat down before him, to the moment when Mouni arrived, Bhagavan's eyes were on you all the time. Not for a moment did he shift his gaze. I was watching you and Bhagavan all the time, and I could see the effect of Bhagavan's look on your mind. Bhagavan has been extremely gracious to you today. He has showered his Grace on you, through the uninterrupted gaze. You have attained the ultimate point of your life today! What more can you want!" I was in no state to say anything at all. I was unable to respond to Kameswaramma's words, because I was in a state beyond speech. The state of my mind was indescribable. I felt a deep peace within me. The outward physical sign of this mental state was the steady flow of the tears that streamed down my cheeks. For many days afterwards, this peace stayed with me. Every time I think about that day's experience, I feel the same thrill of ecstasy.

Most spiritual teachers attach a lot of importance to the initiation ceremony. But that was not Bhagavan's way. He never gave formal initiation to anybody. Nevertheless, he wrought miracles with a mere look. Many of his devotees have had experiences very similar to mine. They can all testify to the power of Bhagavan's 'Glance of Grace'. Through a mere look, Bhagavan could transform a person's mind and heart. Through the Grace that flowed from his eyes, a person could transcend all obstacles and enter the realms of Supreme Bliss, without any conscious personal effort.

13. CASHEWNUTS

On the 1st of September, 1946, the 50th anniversary of Bhagavan's arrival in Tiruvannamalai was celebrated with a grand function to mark the occasion. Special pujas were also performed. A large hall with a thatched roof was constructed, and this hall served as the venue for all the functions connected with the celebrations. This hall, situated to the west of the old meditation hall, came to be known as the Jubilee Hall.

After the completion of the Golden Jubilee celebrations, Bhagavan used to spend a large part of the day in the Jubilee

Hall itself. This was because the old hall had become too cramped. Sri Ramanasramam was attracting more and more people every day and sometimes, the old hall just could not accommodate all the visitors. Some had to sit in the outer verandah, or just outside the window on the western wall. The Jubilee Hall, being large and spacious, could accommodate a large number of people. Moreover, Bhagavan's special friends (peacocks and monkeys, squirrels and dogs) could come and visit him much more easily!

Once in a while, someone or the other would bring some light snacks to the Ashram. Around 3 o'clock in the afternoon, Bhagavan would sample a little of these snacks and have the rest distributed among the devotees in the hall. Somehow, I developed a desire to bring something for this afternoon snack time. But I had a big problem. I did not possess the facilities to prepare a sufficient quantity of any eatable. My room was a tiny one and all my vessels were also rather small. I was living alone and I was not equipped for any bulk preparations. The desire to take some snacks to the Ashram however, remained strong. After a few days of intense thought, I hit upon a solution to the dilemma. I asked a friend to get some cashewnuts from Tiruvannamalai Town. With the money I gave him, he purchased about 1 Kg. of cashewnuts for me. I requested my landlady, Komutti Lakshmi Ammal to let me use her kitchen. She was kind enough to lend me her own vessels. I roasted the cashewnuts in ghee, added salt and pepper powder, and put them in a container and took it to the Ashram.

I am very shy by nature and had never been able to approach Bhagavan with ease and familiarity, the way many of the devotees did. I had no idea about what to do in the present situation. How was I to approach Bhagavan? What if anything, should I say? If he were to ask me why I had taken the trouble to prepare something, how was I to answer him? These doubts plagued me all the way to the Ashram.

I reached the Jubilee Hall and found the courage to walk up to Bhagavan's sofa. There was quite a crowd in the Hall. Bhagavan was reclining on the sofa, and a large number of men and women sat in front of him, imbibing the grace that flowed from him in a steady stream. My hesitation grew when I saw the size of the gathering. But I managed to overcome my timidity and made my way through the crowd. When I reached Bhagavan's side, I found that my heart was beating wildly, and I could not speak. Wordlessly, I held out my offering. Bhagavan looked at me kindly and asked, "What have you brought?" I managed to say, "I have brought some cashewnuts," but I doubt whether Bhagavan could have heard me at all, as my voice was very low, and my speech quite indistinct. Bhagavan craned his neck and looked into the vessel I was holding out. He said, "Oh! Cashewnuts, is it?" and nodded his head at me. Then he said to the attendant, Sathyanandam, "Please take it from her and keep it aside." Looking at me, he said, "Give the vessel to him." I did as I was told and after prostrating to Bhagavan, I went and sat down in my usual place.

I had been hoping that Bhagavan would take a few of my cashewnuts and then have the rest distributed among the gathering. That was the usual procedure after all! I waited eagerly for Bhagavan to accept my offering. But he did not even touch the container- leave alone taste the cashewnuts I had prepared with such eager devotion. I could not understand it at all. Had I done something wrong? Was Bhagavan displeased with me, for some reason? My mind was in turmoil. I felt utterly miserable and tears ran down my face. With a great effort, I forced myself to stop crying. I said to myself, 'This is my fate. I must accept it.' I managed to keep to my usual routine. I stayed till the evening recitation was over and returned home after that. Throughout the night, I was restless. My mind kept going over and over the incident, and I had no peace at all.

The next morning, I reached the Ahram in time for the 5 o'clock veda recitation. After the recitation, I returned home, finished my cooking, and then went back to the Ashram at about 7.30. There was not much of a crowd in the Hall at that time. I went up to Bhagavan and prostrated. As soon as I got up, Bhagavan turned to Sathyanandam and enquired, "Has she been told that the cashewnuts were served along with the iddlies (rice cakes) at breakfast time?" Sathyanandam replied, "I have not told her yet." Then Bhagavan looked at me and said, "They were served along with the iddlies." There was an expression of infinite compassion on Bhagavan's face as he looked at me. I felt a thrill pass through my body. My heart was full. I felt that the sheer happiness of the moment was more than adequate compensation for the misery of the previous day.

Later, Venkataratnam said to me, "*Akka* (sister)! Yesterday, there were many people here. Maybe Bhagavan felt that there might not be enough cashewnuts for everybody. That must be why he had them put away. This morning, all of us were able to enjoy the delicacy you had prepared." Yes. That must have been the reason. In my foolishness, I had been unable to understand. Bhagavan was not displeased with me at all! On the contrary, I had recieved his grace in full measure. All my doubts and fears vanished, and my mind regained the tranquility that had been temporarily lost.

14. The Telegram

Even though my parents agreed to let me stay in Tiruvannamalai, they were very much concerned about my wellbeing. They felt that I was too young and inexperienced to live all alone so far away from the rest of the family. Seeing the strength of my resolve, they were forced to let me go, but they were not really reconciled to the situation. Just before I left home, my father said to me, "You are going to Ramanasramam to follow your spiritual pursuits under the guidance of Bhagavan. You have my blessings. But before you go, I would like you to promise me something. If ever I send for you, you should not hesitate to come home." I knew that my father's affection and concern for me were the reason for his extracting such a promise from me. So I agreed to his condition, and left for Tiruvannamalai.

As I had stated earlier, I was rather shy by nature, and did not make friends easily. In fact, few people even knew what my mother tongue was. I spoke to no one. I visited nobody. I had no social contacts of any kind.

A few months after my arrival at the Ashram, I got a telegram from my father, telling me that he was not well, and asking me to come home immediately. The news was so shocking that I did not know what to do. I went to see Appu Sastri, who lived in another portion of the same house in which I had my room. Appu Sastri was a disciple of Kavyakanta Ganapati Muni. He was also a family friend of ours, and knew both my father and my uncle quite well.

Appu Sastri read the message and immediately took me to the Ashram. Bhagavan was sitting on the sofa, when we arrived at the Ashram. Appu Sastri went up to Bhagavan and showed him the telegram. Bhagavan read it and said, "Oh! This says that Kanaka's father is sick, and he wants her to come home immediately. Who will take her to the station and put her on the train?" Appu Sastri replied, "I will take care of the arrangements myself, Bhagavan." Bhagavan appeared satisfied with this. He then gave me leave, with a smile.

There are numerous people who would consider it a great privilege to do Bhagavan's bidding. There is no doubt about that. Yet, Bhagavan never called anyone and directly said, "You do this." Bhagavan was always in a state beyond anything that ordinary people can imagine. He made no difference between the doer and the action. Bhagavan could have told Appu Sastri, "You should go to the station and help Kanaka catch the train." But he did not say that. Appu Sastri suggested it himself, and Bhagavan expressed his approval of the idea. How can I describe this extraordinary combination of great compassion and total detachment which was unique to Bhagavan!

After the meeting with Bhagavan, Appu Sastri took me back home. He arranged for a ticket on the train going to Katpadi. The train was scheduled to leave Tiruvannamalai at 6 in the evening. So, he arranged for a bullock cart to take me to the station in time to catch the train. When the cart driver arrived, Appu Sastri helped me to load my luggage into the cart. The driver of the cart was a trustworthy man, whom Appu Sastri knew quite well.

I reached the station, caught the train, and travelled upto Katpadi. At Katpadi, I had to get off and catch another train to reach our hometown. When I reached home, I was relieved to find that my father's condition had improved considerably. He was now out of danger, and was gradually regaining his strength.

Meanwhile, as soon as I had left for the station, a second telegram had arrived at the Ashram. Appu Sastri opened it and read the message: "Father better. You need not come now." At once, Appu Sastri told Bhagavan about it. Bhagavan said, "If this message can be conveyed to Kanaka, she will be able to return to the Ashram. Who will go to the station and give her the message?" One of the devotees present said, "The train would have arrived by now." Bhagavan said, "Is that so? Would it have arrived so soon?" The matter was then dropped, because there was really no point in pursuing it any further. The station is about 2 miles from the Ashram, and moreover, there was no transport available. Even the bullock cart drivers had to be fixed up in advance. Otherwise, it was almost impossible to get any kind of transport, especially in the evening time.

Appu Sastri wrote me a letter giving all these details, and enquiring about my father's health. When I read that letter, I was overcome by emotion. I was moved by this evidence of Bhagavan's concern for me. I felt thrilled that Bhagavan had made such kind enquiries about me, and I longed to get back to the Ashram immediately.

I showed Appu Sastri's letter to my father. After reading it, my father said, "Oh! I am very sorry. I should not have been so hasty. But at first, the situation really appeared quite bad and that is why I wanted you to come at once. But after despatching the telegram, there was some improvement. I thought I should save you the trouble of coming all the way. So I arranged for the second telegram to be sent, hoping it would reach you before you left the Ashram. But it seems to have arrived too late. My dear girl, now that you have come, please stay with us for a few days. We would all love to have you with us for a while."

15. GET UP! GET UP!

Bhagavan used to be seated upon the stone sofa in the new hall in front of the Mother's shrine. Ladies used to sit to the right of Bhagavan's sofa. Bhagavan stretched his legs in that direction and so, we used to feel as though we had been granted the rare privilege of sitting at his lotus feet. I usually sat in the corner near the small door. Bhagavan normally used this door when he left the hall to go to the cowshed.

One morning, I was sitting in my usual spot, deep in meditation. I did not even notice the arrival of Mouni with the day's mail. After going through the letters, Bhagavan got ready to go to the cowshed, as per routine. He massaged his legs with oil, and got down from the sofa. Immediately, all the devotees except me got up and made way for Bhagavan! I was so engrossed in meditation that I was totally unaware of what was going on around me. I continued to sit there, directly in Bhagavan's path. When Bhagavan had come very close to the spot, a lady devotee tapped me on the shoulder and hissed in my ear, "Get up! Get up quickly! Bhagavan has to go out and you are blocking the way." With a violent start, I opened my eyes. My legs had become numb from sitting in the same spot for a long time. So, I was not able to get up immediately. Somehow, I managed to rise, and went to stand against the wall.

Bhagavan had seen all this. He was annoyed with the lady who had told me to get up. He chided her in Telugu, "Where was the need to disturb her? There is so much space here. You need not have woken her at all. Does devotion to Bhagavan mean disturbing other people?"

The lady held me responsible for the fact that Bhagavan had rebuked her. She was angry with me. She grumbled, "Some people like to draw attention to themselves by pretending to be absorbed in meditation." I tried my best to convince her that I had really been unaware of Bhagavan's approach, but she remained sceptical. I was very much upset by the lady's attitude, but I could not do anything about it.

From that time onwards, I never sat in that spot. And I regret to say that Bhagavan never used that particular doorway again. After that incident, Bhagavan started using the eastern doorway. The doorstep on this side was rather high and so, a thick coir mat had to be laid there, to make it easier for Bhagavan to step across. Every time I saw Bhagavan using that doorway, I felt consumed by guilt. I wanted to cry, "I am very sorry, Bhagavan. Please forgive me for having caused you so much trouble. Please start using the smaller door again." But I could never find the courage to actually say all this to Bhagavan. Just looking at Bhagavan rendered me speechless. The other devotees too, hesitated to speak to Bhagavan about this matter. Right upto the end, Bhagavan never used the smaller doorway again.

16. THE TRIAD

My parents and my brothers had great regard for Sri Chandrasekharendra Saraswati Swami, the Sankaracharya of the Kanchi Kamakoti *math*. This sage was revered as 'the Paramacharya'. Whenever the opportunity arose, my father would go to see the Paramacharya and get his blessings. In 1958, the Paramacharya was on a visit to Madras and he was staying in the Aswamedha Mandapam in West Mambalam. One evening, when I went to see him, the Paramacharya was alone in the room except for one or two of the *math* attendants. I was very happy to have the unexpected chance to speak to him without disturbance. I had brought some fruits as offering. I placed the tray of fruits before him and prostrated.

Paramacharya looked at me with a smile and made gracious enquiries about my family members. He then asked me, 'Are you on a visit to Madras?" I nodded my head. Then he said, "Are you not staying in Ramanasramam in Tiruvannamalai?" I replied, "I am a permanent resident there."

Paramacharya's next words gave me a thrill. He said, "**Yours is a life of contemplation in solitude, is it not? (ஏகாந்த வாசமோ?)**" I was unable to speak; I just nodded my head. Then he asked, "**Engaging yourself in listening to Vedantic texts? (வேதாந்த சிரவணமோ?)**" Again I nodded silently. His next question was, "**Are you cooking for yourself? (சுயம்பாகமோ?)**" Once more, I nodded. I was overcome by emotion because, in three succinct questions, Paramacharya had summed up the most significant aspects of my life at that time. I had been living alone for a long time, spending my time in contemplation and meditation. Ever since settling down in Tiruvannamalai, I had cooked my own meals. It was during that period that I had the privilege of listening to Muruganar's exposition of that immortal work, *Ozhivil Odukkam*. Obviously, Paramacharya's three questions gave me an emotional satisfaction beyond description. With tears in my eyes, I prayed, "With Paramacharya's blessings, my life should continue along these same lines." Such is Paramacharya's compassion that he graciously lifted his palm in benediction and said, with a smile, "Yes, alright."

It seemed to me that Paramacharya had wanted to know the details of my life at Ramanasramam. His questions had been unerringly directed at finding out these details. Having obtained this information, he smiled his approval, and with his benedictory gesture, assured me that things would continue unchanged, thus affording me the opportunity to carry on with my spiritual pursuits. Such is the power of his look that I felt totally convinced that my spiritual pursuits would proceed satisfactorily, now that I had obtained the seal of approval from Paramacharya himself.

17. It is All the Same

As mentioned earlier, my parents were rather orthodox in their outlook. All my family members had great regard for the Paramacharya of Kanchi *math*. Spiritual matters have always been given importance in my family. When at the age of twenty-four I decided to make Ramanasramam my permanent home, my relatives were upset. My mother was understandably worried about my physical comfort and security. But she was unable to do anything about it because I enjoyed my father's support, and had his permission to stay at Ramanasramam and engage in spiritual practices. Because of their closeness to the Paramacharya of Kanchi, it is quite likely that my family informed him about my life. Someone or the other might even have requested him to intervene and to use his influence to convince me to lead a 'normal' life. I have visited the Kanchi Acharya on many occasions. Not even once has he criticised my chosen way of life. Not once did he ask me why I could not take up the duties of a married woman.

Whenever I happened to visit him, the Paramacharya always raised his hand in benediction and gave me a smile and a look full of Grace. I took this to mean that he approved of my way of life, and that I had his blessings in full measure. My sister-in- law told me that every time she visited Paramacharya, he would ask her, "How is Ashram Kanaka?" My sister-in-law recounted this to me with obvious pride and hearing about it made me very happy. Once, while on a visit to my grandmother in Kanchipuram, I was able to have darshan of Paramacharya every day. Soon however, it was time for me to return to Ramanasramam. When my grandmother came to know that I was planning to leave soon, she was upset. She wanted me to stay with her for some more time. So she went to Paramacharya and requested him to convince me to stay on in Kanchipuram for some more time. Paramacharya listened to my grandmother patiently. Then, with a smile on his lips, he said, "How does it matter whether she is at Ramanasramam or here in Kanchipuram? It is all the same!" (இங்கேயாகு என்ன! அங்கேயாகு என்ன!)

Paramacharya's words were music to my ears! I was elated because he had openly endorsed my choice. I was moved to tears by this unexpected display of his Grace. Paramacharya's eyes have an indescribable power. A glance of those eyes can electrify a person and thrill him to the very core of his being! No one can remain impervious to the captivating glance of those eyes. Once caught in that mesmerising look, one loses all sense of individuality. The mind automatically turns inwards and one gets a feeling of utter peace. One loses all desire for anything else. All one wants is to stay for ever in his Presence, bathed in the endless shower of his Grace!

18. The Sage of Kanchi

All of us should consider ourselves fortunate for having been born during the time that the great sage of Kanchipuram, the Paramacharya, lived on this earth. He is undoubtedly one of the greatest sages of this era. He provided guidance and solace to the thousands who flocked to have his darshan. The compassion in his glance, and the sense of security generated by the sight of his palm raised in a gesture of blessing, made an indelible impression on the mind of every devotee.

It was around 1956. I had gone to see the Paramacharya. At that time, he was staying in 'Little' Kanchipuram (a small village close to Kanchipuram Town). When I reached the place, I found Paramacharya sitting on the floor, leaning against a pillar. I went close and prostrated to him. Paramacharya gestured towards a spot nearby, and asked me to sit there.

Many people came to Paramacharya that day. Almost everybody had some problem or the other, and had come to Paramacharya to seek solace and to obtain his blessings. Curiously enough, every single problem was of a purely worldly nature. Some people complained about their children neglecting them, some told Paramacharya about the diseases they were suffering from, and the difficulties they were forced to put up with. Others wanted Paramacharya's blessings for the marriage of a daughter or for the career of a son. Paramacharya listened to every single petitioner and blessed them all with a compassionate look and with his hand raised in benediction. I was watching all this from the spot assigned to me. I had no idea why Paramacharya had asked me to wait. I was even more puzzled because he seemed to have forgotten all about me. After a while, the crowd thinned down noticeably. The stream of visitors slowed to a mere trickle.

When there was nobody nearby, Paramacharya turned to me and asked, "Do you know what they call me?" I was taken aback by this unexpected and unusual question. I did not know what to say. Finally, I managed to stammer, "You are known as Sankaracharya Swami." Paramacharya replied, "No. I am called the Jagadguru, the Preceptor of Advaita philosophy. But who is bothered about all that!" Though Paramacharya said this with a whimsical smile, the irony of the situation affected me strongly. Here was a sage and a scholar, a Preceptor beyond compare, the Master who could lead us all on a voyage of spiritual discovery. But we, in our ignorance, squander away this unique opportunity, never rising above the petty concerns of everyday life.

On another occasion, I saw another facet of Paramacharya. He was staying in the Sanskrit College in Madras. Every day, hundreds of devotees came to take his blessings. One day, an advocate who was very close to Paramacharya approached him and said, "Paramacharya continues to give *darshan* to devotees almost till midnight, and the next day begins at 4 a.m." Paramacharya looked at his devotee standing before him with moist eyes and folded palms. With a sweet smile full of compassion, he said, "What can I do? These people come to me in the belief that I can help them. They seem to think that if they tell me about their troubles, I can help them find solutions. That is why they come to me at all hours of the day or night. Talking to me gives them confidence and hope. By lightening their burdens, am I not helping them in some way? That is enough for me. It does not matter if I do not get much rest. The satisfaction that comes from helping the people is refreshing enough for me!"

It is an indisputable fact that people have come to Paramacharya with terrible tales of affliction and intolerable sufferings, and have found that once they had obtained Paramacharya's blessings, their troubles disappeared miraculously. Paramacharya is indeed, Divinity in human form!

19. Pilgrimage to Badrinath

When the Kanchi Paramacharya was camping at the Sanskrit College premises in Madras, my mother, grandmother, my elder brother and his son were all planning a pilgrimage to the shrine of Badrinath. I was not very keen on going with them because I had already been to Badri with Dr. T.M.P. Mahadevan, Swami Rajeshwarananda and some others, just two years earlier.

My grandmother and the others went to the Paramacharya to obtain his blessings for the proposed pilgrimage. Paramacharya asked them a number of questions regarding their plans. When he had obtained all the details of the itinerary, he asked, "Isn't Kanaka going with you?" My mother replied, "Kanaka has already been to all these places and so she is not particularly eager to come with us now." When he heard this, Paramacharya sent one of his attendants to our house to fetch me. I hurried to the Sanskrit College in response to the summons. Paramacharya smiled at me and said, "When people visit a place for the first time, they feel unsure of themselves in the unfamiliar conditions. They might not know which spots are worth visiting, and might miss out something important. Moreover, your mother and your grandmother are quite old, and would be glad to have you with them. You can prove to be of assistance to everybody, and your experience could benefit them all. So you must go with them on this trip." When Paramacharya said this, I had no choice but to agree. Paramacharya looked at my grandmother and said, "Kanaka will be able to guide you and to make sure that you visit all the important places. My blessings are with you. Have a safe and comfortable trip!" My grandmother was overjoyed.

The next morning, when I went to the Sanskrit College for my regular *darshan*, there were very few persons there. Paramacharya made kind enquiries, smiled at me and said, "I want you to find out all about the presiding deity in every temple you visit, as well as the name of the sacred river that flows through each town. Will you give me all these details after your return from the pilgrimage?" I felt a little apprehensive about fulfilling this assignment to his satisfaction, but I replied, with all the confidence I could muster, "I will do my best to gather all the information."

With the Paramacharya's blessings, we started out on our pilgrimage. We went to Kurukshetra via Delhi. We reached Kurukshetra on the New Moon day of the Tamil month of Aadi. This day is considered eminently suitable for the offering of oblations to one's ancestors. We bathed in the sacred River Jyothisara, and performed the prescribed rituals. From Kurukshetra, we went to Haridwar and Rishikesh and proceeded to Badrinath. After worshipping at the Badrinath Shrine, we came to Kasi (Benares). We stayed in Benares for ten days. During our stay in Benares, a number of religious ceremonies were performed. Then we visited Gaya, Allahabad and Ayodhya and went on to Ujjain.

We visited the shrines of Mahakaleswar and Siddheswari. Then we went to a few places nearby, like Avanthi, Sudamapuri, Sandeepani and Gomathikund. From there we went to Baroda, via Onkaram. Next was Ahmedabad, from where we went to Junaghat, passing Rajkot on the way. After visiting Dwaraka, Pet

Dwaraka, Balkatheerth etc., we went to Somnath, which is one of the twelve most sacred shrines of Lord Siva (*Dwadasa-Linga Kshetra*).

The next stop was Nasik. From Nasik, we went to Triambak and then climbed the mountains to reach the spot where the River Godavari originates. We also visited the shrine of Gorakhnath, a great saint. We then proceeded to Bombay. We did a bit of sight-seeing in Bombay, visited the Mahalakshmi Temple and some other places. Then we returned to Madras. With Paramacharya's blessings, the entire trip passed off without any problems or illnesses. As soon as we reached home, we went to see the Paramacharya. We took the sacred water of the Ganges, the sandalwood paste from the Badrinath Temple, the sacred ash and the kumkum (vermilion powder) from the various temples, and some fruits and flowers with us. We placed the tray in front of the Paramacharya and prostrated to him.

Paramacharya made gracious enquiries about our trip. When he asked my grandmother, "Did you have a comfortable journey? Are you satisfied with the experience?", she nearly broke down. Indeed, we had a remarkably trouble-free pilgrimage. My grandmother was 93 years old at that time. She and my mother were very orthodox. Inspite of all these restrictions and complications, our trip was free of hitches. Surely this was because of Paramacharya's blessings! Two days later, Paramacharya sent one of the *math* attendants to fetch me. Paramacharya was seated behind a bamboo screen and was surrounded by a large crowd of devotees. I waited for a long time, but could not catch his attention. Finally, I approached Sri Vedapuri, a relative of ours who was one of the *math* attendants, and asked him to inform Paramacharya about my presence in the hall. As soon as the information reached him, Paramacharya sent for me. I went and prostrated to him.

He started questioning me about all the places we had visited on our pilgrimage. He asked me the name of the Presiding Deity in each of the temples we had been to, the names of the holy rivers in the area, and all other details regarding the various pilgrim centres.

In a place close to Ujjain, there is a pipul tree with the figure of Lord Anjaneya clearly visible on its trunk. It looks as though the figure has grown out of the tree itself. All pilgrims make it a point to go and see the marvellous sight of Lord Anjaneya on a tree- trunk. This tree is in a forest by the side of a hill, and a river flows nearby. I asked someone the name of the river and was told that it was the River Vipra. When he heard this, the Paramacharya said, "What did you say? Tell me again!" When I repeated that the river was called Vipra, He said, "Maybe the local people call it Vipra, but the real name is River Shipra."

Then the Paramacharya asked me, "How did you feel when you were standing before Lord Mahakaleswar in the Ujjain Temple?" This question stunned me, because I had had a unique experience in that place. That the Paramacharya should have chosen to question me about that particular moment seemed nothing short of a miracle!

Upon reaching the Mahakaleswara Temple in Ujjain, we first had a dip in the sacred tank. Then we entered the shrine of the Lord. We had already made arrangements for the performance of *abhishekam* to the deity. My mother, grandmother, brother and nephew were all seated around the Linga in the sanctum, and were performing the *abhishekam* under the guidance of the *Panda* (priest). I did not join my relatives because, the moment I entered the shrine, I felt an irresistible force drawing me to the deity. I lost all sense of time and space, and my mind was empty of thoughts of any kind. All I could do was to lean against the wall and gaze at the idol of Lord Mahakaleswara. My relatives called me and asked me to join them, but I was powerless to respond to their calls. The peace I felt at that time is beyond description. The experience was so profound that even after we had left the place, the peace and the joy of those moments stayed with me.

From the Mahakaleswara temple, we went to the temple of the Goddess Siddheswari. Here, devotees were reciting verses from the Devi Mahathmiyam. That was also a very fulfilling experience. That the Paramacharya should ask about the most poignant moments of the long pilgrimage is certainly no mere coincidence. There is nothing so secret, no experience so private that a realised soul cannot know about it.

The Paramacharya's question had been so unexpected, and I was so incapable of expressing my feelings that I could only mumble, "I do not know how to describe my experience." The Paramacharya understood me and blessed me with his raised palm and with a smile full of compassion and understanding.

20. HEART MAY RULE THE MIND

When Bhagavan left the body, his devotees were desolate. Our grief was intolerable, and we were unable to carry on with our lives the way we had done before. In the hope of regaining some degree of mental composure, we requested Muruganar to explain Bhagavan's *Collected Works*. Accordingly, Muruganar started his lectures on the *Collected Works*. These lectures went on for about six months. Muruganar was an exceptional teacher. His lectures were notable for their clarity and for the wealth of illustrations, quotations and allusions to other philosophical works. Sometimes, the explanation of a single stanza could take two or three days. Muruganar was able to make us understand the most intricate poetry and to grasp the real meaning of Bhagavan's teachings.

Once the *Collected Works* had been discussed fully, Sri Muruganar started taking classes exclusively for me. One of the works he explained to me is the *Ozhivil Odukkam*. Sri Muruganar used to say that this was one of Bhagavan's favourite books. Muruganar told me that the existing commentary for this book was based on *Siddhanta* and that Bhagavan had asked him to write another commentary for the book, based on *Vedanta*. Muruganar, however, was unable to carry out the assignment Bhagavan had set. During his lectures on the *Collected Works*, Muruganar often quoted from *Ozhivil Odukkam*. These verses were extremely sweet and moving. I was so charmed by the verses recited by Muruganar that I developed the desire to read the work in its entirety. But it is a very complex work, totally beyond my grasp. Tamil language allows for the combination of words to form complex word-chains. Unless one knows how to break up these word-chains, it is impossible to understand anything. One requires the guidance of an experienced teacher to comprehend this work. Muruganar graciously agreed to be my teacher.

Muruganar's method of teaching was as revolutionary as it was effective. He would insist upon my reading each verse aloud. Unfamiliar as I was with the intricacies of the language, my attempts at reading were quite clumsy and often totally confusing! But my teacher was very patient with me. After my faltering attempts at reading the verse, he would read the same verse, splitting the words properly and pausing at the appropriate places. When Muruganar read a verse, even I could get the broad outlines of its meaning. He would read each verse four or five times. I would unconsciously memorise the verse, even as Muruganar read it. Next, he would set about explaining it to me. He would quote extensively from great works like *Tirumandiram, Tiruvachakam, Tirukkural* and *Naaladiyar.* At times, I felt quite bewildered by the profusion of information that seemed to be swirling around my head!

My difficulties could not have escaped his attention. This great scholar had the compassion to come down to my level and to teach me the rudiments of grammar, so that I could appreciate the poetry better. He would explain the rules which governed the combination of words, and train me to read the poetry the way it was meant to be read.

At the end of one of our classes, I said, "Swami! I very much regret the fact that I am not quite familiar with the Tamil language. If only I had known the language, I could have memorised all these verses without much difficulty. I feel that I am not a pupil worthy of a teacher of your calibre. I am really very sorry." Muruganar replied, "It does not matter if these lessons do not leave an impression upon your brain. It is enough if your heart is genuinely moved by the poetry." Even as he said these words, my teacher's eyes filled with tears and his voice became hoarse with emotion. Needless to say, he himself had experienced that state of total emotional involvement with such spirited works and it is a measure of his infinite grace that he should have wished me to have an experience similar to his own.

21. Self is Everywhere

One day, there was a *sadhu* (ascetic) among the gathering of devotees in the Hall. From his very appearance, it was obvious that he was deep into spiritual practices. It looked as though he was waiting for an opportunity to ask Bhagavan something. When he felt that the time was right, the Sadhu approached Bhagavan and said, "Bhagavan! It is said that the Self (Atman) is present in everything. Does that mean that the Self is to be found, even in a dead body?"

When he heard this, Bhagavan exclaimed, "Oh! This is what you want, is it? Is it the dead body who wants to know, or is it you? Who is asking this question?" The Sadhu replied, "It is I who want to know, Bhagavan." Then, Bhagavan said, "While you are asleep, do you wonder, 'Am I here or not?' It is only in the wakeful state that you say, 'I am'. Similarly, the Self is definitely present even in a dead body. But if you enquire further, you will realise that both the dead body and the living body are both equally illusory. That which moves, we label as being 'alive', and that which is motionless, we say is 'dead'. This differentiation is only in our minds. In our dreams, we see both the 'living' and the 'dead'. As soon as we wake up, we realise that both the 'living' and the 'dead' of our dreams are but illusions. In the same way, this entire universe is nothing more than a grand illusion. The birth of the 'I thought' is referred to as 'birth', and the disappearance of the 'I thought' is 'death'. What we call 'birth' and 'death', therefore, are nothing but the appearance and disappearance of the 'I thought'. Both birth and death are for the ego alone. Neither 'birth' nor 'death' can touch the 'I' which forms the essence of your being. When the awareness of the self is strong, you are there; you are equally there when the self-awareness fades. It is 'you' that is the source of the 'I-thought'. But the 'I-thought' is not you. Realization is nothing but perceiving the source of the cycle of birth and death, and uprooting the ego and destroying it completely. That is, you must 'die' and still remain aware. He who 'dies' with awareness is transformed into pure Self. That is, when the ego dies, the Self is born. When this happens, all doubts vanish immediately. The veil of illusion is lifted and everything is perceived properly. All confusion is removed. The differentiations between birth and death, living and dead, everything disappears. The Self is all-knowing. The Self has no doubts. It is only the ego that is plagued by doubts."

On hearing this explanation, the Sadhu's face glowed with understanding. It was obvious that he had finally found the answer to the question that had obviously bothered him for a long time. Can such a wonderful lesson be learned from any book? Only Bhagavan could give such a clear, concise and convincing reply to such a question.

22. BHAGAVAN'S WIT

Bhagavan had a marvellous sense of humour. His sense of timing was perfect. Every word was suited to the occasion, and even the seemingly casual utterances were gems of wit and wisdom. Bhagavan possessed the unique ability to convey the most profound truths in the simplest language. He conversed with great scholars and illiterate peasants with equal ease. He adapted his language and his style to suit the requirements and the capacity of the listeners. Bhagavan's teachings made an indelible impression on the listener's mind, because his words were always exquisitely appropriate, effectively direct and unambiguously clear. Even when apparently speaking in jest, Bhagavan conveyed valuable messages to the devotees around him. With some people he was very gentle and with some he was witty and playful. At all times and with all people however, his words were full of meaning. Even when he seemed to be teasing a devotee, or gently poking fun at somebody, Bhagavan's words contained profound truths, and served as valuable lessons for his disciples. I shall recount some interesting instances which highlight Bhagavan's felicity of language and his inimitably nimble wit.

Once Bhagavan happened to spend quite a long time with a particular devotee. For nearly two hours at a stretch Bhagavan was sitting in the same position. When it was time for Bhagavan's daily visit to the cowshed, an attendant came and stood at the entrance to the hall, holding Bhagavan's walking stick and the *Kamandal* (water jug) in his hands. Seeing the attendant standing ready, Bhagavan tried to get up. But his legs had grown numb from sitting in the same position for a long time, and Bhagavan could not get up immediately.

Bhagavan smiled at the waiting attendant and said, "Wait a minute! The father of the greatest devotee of Lord Rama (Anjaneya) has caught hold of my legs. He is not an ordinary person. Will he set me free so easily? I can pull myself out of his grip only a little at a time. So you will have to wait patiently for a while!" While he spoke, Bhagavan was rubbing a medicinal oil on his knees, and as a result of the massage, he was able to get up and go out. The devotees in the hall were amused by Bhagavan's words. Bhagavan was prone to painful arthritic attacks, especially in the knee joints. According to some principles of medicine, pain in the joints is caused by the trapping of wind in those spots. When Bhagavan talked about 'the father of the devotee of Rama' he meant Vayu, the Wind-God, who is the father of Anjaneya. Instead of simply saying, 'There is a painful catch in my knee', Bhagavan had chosen to convey the same information in a humorous way.

On another occasion, while rubbing the oil on his knees, Bhagavan looked up with a mischievous glint in his eyes and said, "This machine (the body) will not run if it is not properly oiled!" All those present had a hearty laugh. Bhagavan's humour was often directed at himself. At times, he used humorous language to rebuke someone. This was done so gently and with such subtlety that the message was conveyed, but the subject of Bhagavan's rebuke was not even slightly hurt or offended.

Bhagavan's attendants used to massage his legs, to relieve the pain. Somehow, a kind of rivalry arose among the attendants. In the belief that by touching Bhagavan's feet and legs, they could acquire a lot of *punya* (merit), the attendants started vying with each other for the privilege of massaging his legs. One day, when two or three of them rushed to offer to massage his legs, Bhagavan exclaimed, "Wait! Wait! Why should you people alone enjoy the entire merit? Allow me to acquire some *punya*, too!" So saying, Bhagavan started massaging his own legs, sending us into peels of laughter.

23. THE STONE GOD

The spacious hall in front of the Matrubhuteswara Temple was built because the old meditation hall was found to be too small for the large crowds that came to the Ashram everyday. As soon as the new hall was completed, Bhagavan was brought there in a ceremonial procession. A group of *Vedic* scholars waited for Bhagavan in front of the *Veda Patasala*. As soon as Bhagavan came out of the cow shed, they started reciting the *Veda mantras*. They welcomed Bhagavan with *Purnakumbham* (ceremonial presentation of vessel filled with sacred water, a traditional way of welcome) and brought him to the new hall. Here a beautiful sofa carved out of black granite had been constructed. Bhagavan was requested to sit on the sofa and he graciously obliged. Amidst the ringing of bells and the burning of incense, the entire gathering of devoteees chanted 'Na Karmana' *mantra* and prostrated before Bhagavan. It was as though a great emperor was holding court in his royal palace.

Soon after Bhagavan had settled himself on the seat, a group of people entered the hall. The Sthapati (the temple sculptor) was holding a tray with fruits, flowers and coconuts. Bhagavan was asked to bless these by touching them. Then they all prostrated to Bhagavan, and taking the tray with them, they went out through the southern door. We had no idea about what was going on. Bhagavan was watching them intently. The devotees too were intrigued and unable to bear the suspense, trooped out of the hall. They were just in time to see the Sthapati performing puja to a large decorated rock in the open space in front of the hall. He then started chipping away with his chisel. Venkatratnam was standing beside me. I asked him what was going on. He said that the Sthapati was going to make a statue of Bhagavan. Bhagavan was ill at that time. The cancer had started its attack. Somehow the idea of making a statue at such a time upset me badly. Bhagavan jocularly remakred, "The stone God is getting ready to sit upon the stone sofa."

* * *

One day, an old gentleman approached Bhagavan and said, "Swami! Please clear my doubts." Bhagavan took one look at this person and started acting like a schoolboy who had not done his homework. Everyone was puzzled by Bhagavan's imitation of a trembling schoolboy. Bhagavan laughed and explained the situation to us. He said, "Do you know who this gentleman is ?   It is only because I could not answer his questions that I ran away from Madurai! I thought I had escaped from him, but he has followed me all the way and is asking questions again!"

The old gentleman was none other than the teacher who had taught Tamil while Bhagavan was in school. Presumably, Bhagavan dreaded being asked questions in class; and here was the same person, once again bent upon posing questions! All of us, including Bhagavan's former teacher, were very much amused by the irony of the situation!

24. Nayana and Namam

Bhagavan used a walking stick, because arthritis made it difficult for him to walk without support. As he adhered to a strict daily routine, his attendants always knew exactly when he would be leaving the hall. So they would bring the walking stick and help Bhagavan out of the hall at the fixed hours. Once, when Bhagavan saw an attendant approaching the hall with the walking stick in his hand, he said to us with a twinkle in his eyes, "Look! Here comes my walking stick! You have seen the monkey trainer teaching his monkeys to dance at the sight of the stick. This monkey must now start dancing, for the stick is here!"*

* * *

---

* The proverb in Tamil is கோலெடுத்தால் குரங்காடும், i.e., as the trainer raises the stick the monkey dances to his tune.

The doctors had advised the Ashram authorities to give Bhagavan some vitamin-rich foods for his arthritis problem. Bhagavan's attendants started preparing special food for Bhagavan and as recounted earlier, were also regularly massaging his legs. Bhagavan did not enjoy all this attention. He used to say, "If an uninvited guest arrives and makes a nuisance of himself, the best way to make him pack-up is to ignore him totally. If we are attentive to him, he will never leave us. In the same way, the more fuss we make over a disease, the longer will it stay with us. The best way to make a disease disappear is to ignore it."

* * *

Once Bhagavan was telling us all about some of the interesting incidents that occurred before the ashram was built. This is one such anecdote. "Rangaswamy Iyengar, a *Vaishnavite* devoteez had a peculiar desire. He wanted to see me wearing the *Namam* (the traditional mark a *Vaishnavite* puts on his forehead). He kept on repeating that it would be good to see Bhagavan wearing a *Namam*. After a while, I said to him, 'Alright! I will do it to please you, but only on one condition. You must make Nayana (as Ganapati Muni was known) wear a *Namam* first. If Nayana does it, I will follow suit.' The red and white chalks were placed beside Nayana's dinner plate that evening by Rangaswamy Iyengar. When Nayana sat down to eat, he became involved in an engrossing dialogue with me. Without even being conscious of doing so, Nayana picked up the chalks and applied the *Namam* on his forehead! As soon as he did so, I too did the same. Shortly, Nayana noticed the *Namam* on my forehead and exclaimed, 'What is this, Bhagavan! Since when did you start this practice?' I replied, 'I saw you wearing a *Namam* and felt that I too should have one.' Nayana was totally taken aback. He said, "What, me?" and looked into the mirror. When he saw himself in the mirror, he was stunned."Saying this, Bhagavan broke into laughter and we all joined him.

* * *

A group of people had come to the Ashram to see Bhagavan. Among them there was a lady of about sixty. She was a widow. Bhagavan gave her a keen look and started laughing, at which the lady became slightly shy. "Oh, it is you!" he said and laughed again at her embarrassment. We were all puzzled. Bhagavan said, "Do you know who this is? When we were children, we used to live in adjacent portions of the same house. In those days, I used to help my mother in the kitchen, wearing just a loin-cloth for reasons of orthodoxy. People around used to say that I must marry the girl next door. The little girl's mother would immediately retort, 'Why should my daughter marry a boy who is not ashamed to work in the kitchen like a girl, and that too, wearing nothing more than a loin-cloth? She deserves someone better.' Fortunately for me, I was not destined to get married at all. If things had been different, and I had married this lady, what would have happened to me!" Bhagavan stated this with a mischievous twinkle in his eye.

25. Mind Your Own Business

One day, one of the devotees came to Bhagavan and said in an excited whisper, "Look, Bhagavan! Just look at that man!" Everyone turned to look. We saw a gentleman who was asleep, swaying back and forth. The gentleman who had approached Bhagavan complained, "I have been watching him for the past few days. He always sleeps in Bhagavan's presence!" Bhagavan looked at the devotee and said, "That man is doing what he came here to do. But what about you? Did you come here just to check on people, and see who is awake and who is asleep? Why don't you mind your own business?" Seeing the over-zealous devotee rebuked like this, all the others were burst out laughing. Bhagavan did not like it at all when people complained about others. He used to say that as long as a person concentrated upon the work he was engaged in, he would not even notice what others were doing. One can find the time to criticise others only when one's own attention wandered from the work at hand.

* * *

Vaikunta Vasan was one of Bhagavan's personal attendants. Literally translated, the name means 'one who resides in Vaikunta', and is one of the names of Lord Mahavishnu. One night, Vaikuntavasan was lying in the hall, next to Bhagavan. Suddenly, he saw a large cobra very close to his pillow. Speechless with terror, Vaikuntavasan turned to Bhagavan and pointed out the snake to him. Bhagavan shouted like a happy little boy, "Look! This is such a beautiful creature, Vaikuntavasa! This is after all your mattress and has come in search of you!" In spite of his terror, Vaikuntavasan burst out laughing. (According to Hindu mythology, Lord Vishnu, the Lord of Vaikunta, reclines upon the great coiled serpent, Adisesha.)

26. ANANDAMMAL

Anandammal was one of Bhagavan's earliest devotees. She came to Bhagavan while he was in Virupaksha Cave. Anandammal's parents had settled down in Tiruvannamalai and the girl's childhood was spent in the temple town. Right from her childhood, she had a spiritual bent of mind. Even as a young girl, she used to come to the Virupaksha Cave very often and sit in meditation before Bhagavan for long periods of time.

When Anandammal reached marriageable age, her parents started looking for a suitable bridegroom. Anandammal had no desire for family life and tried her best to dissuade her parents from getting her married. But her protests were in vain and she had to get married.

Even after her marriage however, she used to go to the Virupaksha Cave every evening and spend her time in blissful meditation in Bhagavan's presence. Her people did not approve of this. They tried to change her ways saying, "Now you are a married woman and your duty is to look after your husband and home. You should not go out every evening." To this Anandammal had only one reply, "I told you that I was not interested in marriage. Why did you not listen to me then?"

In course of time Anandammal gave birth to a son. Her relatives rejoiced, thinking that the child would bind her more firmly to her home life. But they were sadly mistaken. She did not allow the birth of her child to interfere with her spiritual pursuits. She left her son in the care of other family members and continued her spiritual practices. After a while, her husband passed away. By this time, Bhagavan had come down from the hill and Sri Ramanasramam had been established. Anandammal came to live in a small thatched hut in Ramananagar. Her brother took up the responsibility of caring for her son. He educated the boy and eventually made him his son-in-law. Anandammal's son and daughter-in-law worked as teachers in a school in Tiruvannamalai town. Anandammal did not attach importance to material possessions or physical needs. A kind hearted lady called Dhanam took upon herself the responsibility of cooking for her and generally looking after her.

Anandammal had not had much education. She was therefore unable to read much even though she was very much interested in philosophical works. A lady from Madurai used to visit Anandammal frequently. This lady was a teacher in Madurai and would come to Sri Ramanasramam during school holidays. She had great respect and love for Anandammal. She would bring good books on philosophical subjects from the library and read them aloud to Anandammal. This lady from Madurai was a Tamil scholar but sometimes she had difficulty in understanding some of the passages in the books she read. Every time she found a passage too difficult to grasp, Anandammal would clear her doubts with concise explanations. The lady was often surprised by Anandammal's intuitive grasp of great philosophical truths.

Aandammal's life is an excellent illustration of the fact that in spiritual sadhana, experience and intuition play a more important role than mere book knowledge. Anandammal never wasted even a single moment of her time. If she could find someone to read to her, she would have works of Bhagavan and the *Ribhu Gita* or some other philosophical work read out to her. She would at times go on Giripradakshinam. If there was nothing else to do, she would calmly sit and meditate for hours together in Bhagavan's presence. She did not spend time in worldly thoughts.

Her very appearance seemed to indicate her purity. She wore an ochre colored sari. Her shorn head and a necklace of Rudraksha beads gave her the appearance of a sannyasini. She had no interest in worldly matters; even with regard to food, she had no likes or dislikes. She ate only to keep the body and soul together. At times, Dhanam had to go away for three or four days at a stretch. On such occasions, she would cook enough rice to last for a few days and leave it in a pot. Anandammal would eat a little of this rice whenever she felt the need. All of her concentration was on the Self and she did not bother about the trivial details of daily life.

Once, I got the idea that it would be nice to prepare some snacks and distribute them among the sadhus in the Ashram. Accordingly I prepared some *pakodas* (savouries) and made several packages. I distributed the packets to all *sadhus* in the Ashram and went to Anandammal's hut with the last packet. When I reached her place, she beckoned me to come and sit beside her. When she noticed the packet in my hand, she asked, "What is it that you have brought?"

I gave her the parcel and explained the background. She admonished me saying, "Why do you waste your time like this? Where did you get the idea that sadhus need such trifles as snacks and sweets? Don't you ever listen to what Bhagavan says? He has told us all repeatedly that the only thing to do is to be still. And yet, you engage yourself in such totally unnecessary activities. Dhanam has left me some rice in the pot in the corner. There is enough of it to keep me from starving till she returns. I have never felt the need for fancy food and I am sure that the sadhus also feel the same way. I am disappointed in you. You do not seem to realise what a great privilege it is to be allowed to live in Bhagavan's presence. You are so young; you will be able to enjoy this privilege for a long time yet. Do not waste this rare opportunity. Concentrate your energy in the search for the Self and do not fritter it away in such worthless activities."

Her strong words brought me to my senses. I realised how irresponsible I had been. I decided never to make such a mistake in future. Since then, I have not been tempted to do anything of that sort. Even if the impulse arose, I would be reminded of Anandammal's words, and this would keep me from succumbing to temptation.

At times her friends came to her with their troubles. Her advice was always the same. " Why do you waste your time on such unimportant things? What is the point in worrying? Life is like that. There will always be some problem or the other. But you should not let your mind dwell on such things. Forget everything and sit at Bhagavan's feet. He will take care of everything."

Anandammal used to say with pride, "This Arunachala has a unique distinction. It is said that if a woman were to do penance here, her prayers are granted very soon. It was here that Goddess Uma became a part of the Lord. There are no temples for Rama's mother Kausalya or Krishna's mother Devaki. But the mother of our Bhagavan, Alagammal, has been granted this unique privilege. Is not the Mathrubhutheswara temple the greatest proof that women are held in very high esteem in Tiruvannamalai?"

After Bhagavan's Mahasamadhi, many of his devotees left Tiruvannamalai and went to far off places in search of solace. But they could not find peace or comfort anywhere Like a sea-bird which takes flight from a ship is compelled to return to it eventually, so also did Bhagavan's devotees return to the haven of Ramanasramam after a while. Though they came back, they were unable to find the peace they had enjoyed during his lifetime. The sight of Bhagavan's favourite resting places, his few personal belongings and the objects he had looked at or touched, all these brought back poignant memories. The devotees were unable to get over the grief of Bhagavan's departure from the physical body.

It was at this time that Anandammal and a few other devotees approached Muruganar and requested him to read from Bhagavan's collected works and explain the same in detail.

Muruganar agreed, hoping that a detailed study of Bhagavan's teachings would help them all overcome their grief. Muruganar's discourses on Bhagavan's Collected Works (*Nool Thirattu*) were very lucid and illuminating. Those days, when we listened to Muruganar's exposition on Bhagavan's works, were blessed ones. It was an unforgettable experience.

Muruganar systematically took us through all the verses and songs in Bhagavan's collected works. These lectures went on regularly for nearly six months. Even after the lectures were over, Anandammal often visited him for clarifications of her doubts, in various other spiritual works. On one such occasion Anandammal approached Muruganar and asked him, "Is it not true that saint Vamadeva attained supreme knowledge even while he was in his mother's womb?" As she was saying this, she fell down. I was standing nearby at that time. At first I thought that Anandammal was just prostrating to Muruganar. But when, even after a long time she did not get up, I sensed that something was seriously wrong. When I lifted her up, I found that she was unconscious. My friend Padma and I tried to revive Anandammal by sprinkling water on her face. But our efforts were in vain. We sent word to Dhanam and she immediately rushed to the town to inform Anandammal's son. As soon as her son arrived, Anandammal was lifted on to a cart and taken to her son's house. Anandammal continued in the same state of unconsciousness throughout the day and breathed her last that night. She was a devotee par excellence, full of detachment, wisdom and spiritual experience. Even her last thoughts and words were on spiritual matters. The purpose of her life was fulfilled and this ripe soul reached Sri Bhagavan's Lotus Feet. Her son and her brother performed the last rites, in the manner prescribed for the interment of a realised soul.

27. FOR WHOM ARE THE RULES?

In the early days, visitors to Ramanasramam could see Bhagavan at any time. There were no restrictions of any kind. It was only later on, when Bhagavan was growing weak, that the Ashram authorities decided to regulate the *darshan* timings. It was out of concern for his health that the authorities tried to provide Bhagavan with some rest. The decision was taken by the authorities and Bhagavan knew nothing about this.

At first, devotees coming from outside had no idea that new rules had been made. Some of Bhagavan's devotees stayed in nearby towns, and visited the Ashram from time to time. Naturally, these people did not know anything about the rules which had been made while they were away from the Ashram.

Narayana Iyer was one of Bhagavan's regular visitors. He worked as a Sub-registrar in Arni, and used to visit the Ashram every Sunday. He would bring some snacks for Bhagavan and his devotees. This was such a regular practice that once, when Shantammal was talking about preparing some snacks in the Ashram kitchen, Bhagavan said, "Today is Sunday, and Narayana Iyer will bring some snacks for all of us. There is no need for you to trouble yourself today." At about 1 o'clock on a Sunday afternoon, Bhagavan saw Narayana Iyer coming towards the hall, with a parcel of snacks in his hand. Bhagavan waited for him, but he did not enter the hall. When Narayana Iyer was hurrying towards the hall, a devotee stopped him and told him not to go in immediately, but to wait until two o'clock. So, Narayana Iyer went away and returned at three o'clock.

As soon as Narayana Iyer entered the hall, Bhagavan asked him, "Did you not come here at 1o'clock? I saw you through the window and was expecting you to enter the hall any moment, but you did not come. Did you have to go somewhere else?" Narayana Iyer had no idea that Bhagavan was not supposed to know about the new arrangement. So, in all innocence, he said, "Yes Bhagavan, I went away then, and returned just now. The train arrived late today, and I reached the Ashram only at one o'clock. When I was about to come inside, I was informed that Bhagavan rests in the afternoons nowadays, and is not to be disturbed till two o'clock. So I went away and came back just now." Bhagavan listened to him without any comment other than his customary, "Oh! Is that so!" Then Narayana Iyer had a long chat with Bhagavan, during the course of which Bhagavan sampled the *Omappodi* (a crisp savoury snack) that Iyer had brought. That night, after dinner, Narayana Iyer took leave of Bhagavan and returned to Arni.

The next day, Bhagavan came to the hall after lunch. Everything seemed quite normal, till about twelve o'clock. It was a rather hot day, and everybody was puzzled when Bhagavan left the hall and went to sit on the platform outside. His attendants were totally at a loss. They did not know how to ask Bhagavan about his decision to leave the cool comfort of the hall. However, after a while, one of them approached Bhagavan and said, "It is unbearably hot here and the hall is cooler. Would it not be more comfortable for Bhagavan to stay inside, at least till two o'clock, when the heat might come down a little?"

To this, Bhagavan replied, "Oh! Is the sun too hot for Bhagavan? You want your Bhagavan to avoid the heat and recline on his sofa inside the cool hall. What about those who come to see Bhagavan? Does not the same sun shine on them also? Do they not feel the heat? Unmindful of the heat, they come to see me. And what do you do? You send them away saying that Bhagavan should not be disturbed till two o'clock. All right.

You have made the rule and I cannot do anything about it. But you have only decided to keep visitors from entering the hall, is it not? Or have you also made another rule that Bhagavan cannot leave the hall during this period?" The attendants had no reply. They were struck dumb by this rare display of Bhagavan's anger.

Though Bhagavan seemed displeased at this restriction upon the devotees, the devotees themselves started voluntarily regulating their visits, so that Bhagavan could have some rest during the hottest part of the day.

28. WORSHIP THE GOD WITH INCENSE

I came to the Ashram in 1946. I remember that there used to be a recitation of the Vedas in Bhagavan's presence at 5 A.M. every morning. In the Tamil month of Margazhi (December-January) the chanting of the *Vedas* used to be preceded by recitations from some of the Tamil devotional works like *Ramana Sannidhi Murai* and *Tiruvachakam*, etc. This Tamil recitation would be from 4 to 5 A.M. The devotees assembled in the hall by four and Bhagavan would be ready long before that. It would be quite cold in the Jubilee Hall. Yet, Bhagavan would not use any warm clothing, except for a woollen shawl, which he wore over his head and around his shoulders. Bhagavan's bright face with his compassionate eyes and his sweet smile, framed by the shawl, was a great sight to behold. The soul-filling sight of Bhagavan's divine form, with the smell of incense, in the quiet early morning hours, was a truly unforgettable experience.

There used to be a small brazier of coals in front of Bhagavan's sofa. An attendant used to sprinkle incense powder on the glowing coals, every once in a while. From time to time,

Bhagavan would hold out his hands over the coals, to warm his fingers. Even this mundane action appeared indescribably graceful when Bhagavan performed it. As long as the incense powder was sprinkled in moderate quantities, the warmth of the fire and fragrance of the incense used to give us all a sense of comfort. But whenever a bit too much of powder fell on the fire, the smoke would rise up in a dense cloud. As Bhagavan was very close to the fire, the smoke would affect him badly. His eyes would water and he would gasp for breath, with his face reddened by the strain.

Once, when the smoke became too thick and suffocating even for Bhagavan's immense patience, he was forced to comment upon it. Even then, Bhagavan did not lose his sense of humour. He said, looking at the devotees gathered around him, "Yes. That is right. You should worship God like this only. The more incense you burn, the more pleased your God will be. I should be thankful that I am worshipped like this only once every day. Can you imagine the plight of the deity in the temple, who has to put up with this kind of worship at least six times a day! No wonder God manifests Himself in the form of stone idols! The troubles of a God can be appreciated only by another God! Can you imagine the hardship God is subjected to, all in the name of worship and devotion? The devotees only think about various ways of expressing their devotion. They never pause to think about the effect of their puja, on God!

"Being a Swami (god) is difficult indeed. As long as one patiently puts up with all forms of worship, listens to everything the devotees say, eats only what is given as offering, and is available day and night, winter and summer, to suit the devotees' convenience, one's Godliness is accepted as being quite satisfactory. If the Swami were to complain, even when the worship becomes extremely uncomfortable, the devotees say, 'What kind of a Swami is this? He too has likes and dislikes, just like an ordinary man! He too gets angry, and has human feelings. How can he be a God, then!' To be a model Swami, maybe I should stop breathing altogether. I must find some way to remain absolutely still and immobile, not moving even a hand or a leg. And I should never complain, even when over-enthusiastic devotees try to choke me with incense smoke. Such are the impossible standards I am expected to maintain!"

Generally, Bhagavan patiently put up with everything. Even when he felt like drawing the attention of his devotees to certain acts, Bhagavan never lost his sense of humour, or his consideration for not hurting the feelings of others. His criticism, though unmistakable in its clarity, was so gently worded and so aptly timed that the offending parties learnt their lessons and mended their ways, without being hurt.

29. JUST A PIPUL TREE

Pichandi was one of Bhagavan's earliest devotees. He used to visit Bhagavan regularly, right from the Virupaksha Cave days. He was the earliest to present Bhagavan with a blanket. Pichandi's house in Talagiri Street was always open to Bhagavan's devotees and he would press devotees to stay with him for some days. He used to send some rice to the Ashram at periodic intervals.

Pichandi's sister, Janaki Ammal, was also a great devotee of Bhagavan. This lady often went around the Arunachala Hill. Every time she set out for *giripradakshinam*, she would come to the Ashram and after taking Bhagavan's blessings, would continue the *giripradakshinam*. She had great love and regard for

Bhagavan. She would narrate all her troubles and Bhagavan would listen to her patiently. He would console her with soothing words.

One evening, Janaki Ammal came to the Ashram. When she entered the hall, Bhagavan was talking about meditation. There was a lady sitting in deep meditation. Janaki Ammal said to Bhagavan, "You tell newcomers how to meditate. How often have I asked you to initiate me into meditation! But you never granted my request. Every time I come to see you, you enquire about the welfare of all the members of my family. If I come here hungry, you press me to eat in the Ashram. But whenever I ask you to give me spiritual instruction, you just turn a deaf ear. Perhaps you consider that these are enough for me and that I cannot take any more!" Even as she spoke, Janaki Ammal's eyes filled with tears. Bhagavan did not say a single word in reply to her complaints. He gave her a compassionate look. Soon afterwards, Janaki Ammal left the hall saying, "So, you are determined to ignore all my pleas. Let me see how long you continue to be deaf to my prayers."

On another occasion, Janaki Ammal came to the Ashram early in the morning. Bhagavan was in the Jubilee Hall. There were just a few people in the hall at that time. Janaki Ammal prostrated to Bhagavan, went around Bhagavan's sofa, and prostrated once again. Bhagavan did not like such things. But Janaki Ammal had done it on a few previous occasions, and Bhagavan had not openly objected. But on this particular day, Bhagavan said to Janaki Ammal, "Look! If you go around the sofa like this, all the newcomers will think, 'Oh! This must be the normal practice in this place. Maybe we have broken the Ashram rules by not following the practice', and everybody sitting here will get up start going round and round my sofa. And if I object to it, they will only say, 'That lady does it. So why should we not do the same?' Can you imagine the resulting confusion? And what would my situation be? I would be like a Pipul tree", said Bhagavan with a smile.

Janaki Ammal simply remarked, "O Bhagavan! This is all your *lila*", and continued her *giripradakshina*. The next time Janaki Ammal started going around Bhagavan's sofa, one of the attendants in the Hall got irritated. He grumbled, "Look at this lady! How many times has she been told not to do this! Maybe she likes to draw the attention of others." This attendant was critical of her behaviour quite often. Stung by the attendant's words this time, Janaki Ammal retorted, "This man is like a thorn near the tree laden with ripe juicy fruit" (பழுத்த மரத்தின் எதிரில் கொழுத்த முள்ளு), and went her way. Bhagavan heard this exchange of words between the two and, turning to a devotee who was standing nearby, said, "If we keep quiet there is no problem; since we have opened our mouth, our true nature has been revealed."* Bhagavan never spoke ill of anyone, and he did not like it if any of his followers indulged in criticism of others. He corrected their faults through gentle remarks and through the example of his own exemplary courtesy towards one and all.

30. Enough of this Chanting of the Fan

September 1st, 1946 marked the Golden Jubilee of Bhagavan's arrival in Tiruvannamalai. A grand celebration was planned for the occasion. A large number of devotees were expected to attend the function and a thatched hall was built to accommodate the expected gathering. From the time of its construction, Bhagavan spent most of his time in this Jubilee hall. As the number of visitors to the Ashram kept increasing day by day, this spacious hall proved to be convenient for all concerned.

One evening, Bhagavan had gone to the cowshed as usual. Devotees were walking up and down, excitedly calling to one another. Attendants were hurrying here and there. The cause of all this activity was a new table fan! It had been sent down from the Ashram Office, for Bhagavan's personal use, and the attendants were debating with one another about where it should be placed, so that Bhagavan could get the full benefit of the breeze. A number of positions were tried out and rejected. Finally, the fan was placed on a small stool close to Bhagavan's sofa, to everyone's satisfaction. Sri Bhagavan entered the Hall and saw the fan near his sofa and asked, "Who brought this?" The attendants replied, "As it is very hot nowadays, it was felt that Bhagavan would be more comfortable if a fan was provided. So, this fan was sent from the Office. It is hoped that Bhagavan will be gracious enough to make use of this fan." Bhagavan examined the fan from every angle and asked a number of questions about how it worked. He wanted to know which switch would turn it on and which would stop it. When they saw Bhagavan's interest in the fan, the attendants and other devotees were overjoyed. They had been apprehensive lest Bhagavan should summarily reject the fan. When he started questioning them in detail, they felt that Bhagavan definitely liked the idea of having a fan in the Hall. Reassured by Bhagavan's attitude, an attendant switched the fan on. Immediately, the fan started rotating. The breeze from the fan was cool and pleasant. But the accompanying noise certainly was not! Like all table fans of that period, it emitted a high pitched whining noise while in operation.

By this time, the Vedic pundits had arrived and they got ready to start the *Veda Parayanam*. Bhagavan said, "We have listened to the chanting of this fan long enough! Please switch it off now, so that we can listen to the chanting of the Vedas." An attendant pressed the switch to turn off the fan. The blades started slowing down, with a noise like a caged bird fluttering its wings in a desperate attempt to escape! Bhagavan said, "Well! It looks as though this fan can produce more noise than breeze! Please take it back to the Office. The people in the Office are always working hard and they need the fan to keep themselves cool. I am only sitting here. This hand fan is quite enough for me." So saying, Bhagavan sent the fan back to the Office.

This was indeed a disappointment for the devotees who had been hoping that Bhagavan would make use of the fan. But they could not have really expected Bhagavan to act differently! They all knew that Bhagavan never accepted any special treatment. He insisted upon sharing everything equally with all the others. Even during meal times, Bhagavan did not allow any special favours to be shown to him. He ate only what everybody else ate. He would not allow any special dishes to be prepared exclusively for himself. Neither did he allow anyone to serve larger portions of any item on his plate. If he felt that he was being served an unusually large helping of any item, he would say, "See! When the others are being served, the ladle refuses to pick up more than a little. But when it comes to me, it gets filled to capacity! What to do! You have the upper hand. I have to eat what I am given. I have to do as I am told. This is what 'godliness' is all about!" Of course, these gentle words had a telling effect upon the devotees and they were even more effective than harsher rebukes could have been.

31. WHY WASTE THE FLOWERS!

Bhagavan often went on *giripradakshinam* with his devotees. On one such occasion, Tiruchuzhi Lakshmi Ammal was in the group. In Tiruchuzhi, Bhagavan's house was close to Lakshmi Ammal's house, and the children of the two families had grown up together, as close friends. Even in later years, after Bhagavan had settled at Ramanasramam and Lakshmi Ammal happened to visit the Ashram, Bhagavan continued to treat her with the affection and informality of an old friend. Lakshmi Ammal felt overjoyed every time Bhagavan called her by name, and addressed some remark to her.

On this particular day, Bhagavan and his party had reached Sona *Tirtham*, and decided to rest there for some time. As the rest of the party settled down, Lakshmi Ammal, having spotted a flowering tree nearby, started plucking flowers. After resting for a short while, Bhagavan and the others resumed the Giripradakshinam. When Bhagavan saw Lakshmi Ammal plucking the flowers, he approached her and asked, "What are you doing, Lakshmi?" Lakshmi Ammal replied, "I am just plucking flowers for puja, Bhagavan." She had spread a towel on the ground and collected the flowers in it. Pointing to the towel, Bhagavan said, "You already have much flowers. Why pluck more?" To this, Lakshmi Ammal artlessly replied, "There are so many flowers on this tree! I thought it would be better to gather them for the puja, rather than let them all go waste."

Bhagavan said, "So! I suppose you cannot perform puja without a large number of flowers. You have already seen and enjoyed the sight of the tree laden with beautiful flowers. Now you do not care whether anybody else gets a chance to enjoy the same heart-warming sight. Or maybe you have some exclusive rights over this tree. Did you plant it and nurture it yourself, thus making it your own personal property?"

Lakshmi Ammal was stunned by Bhagavan's words. She was full of remorse for her thoughtless action. This incident made such an impression on her mind that, from that moment onwards, she never plucked flowers from plants. Every time she saw a beautiful flower on a bush or a tree, she would mentally dedicate it to God saying, "O Lord! This is Yours. Accept this flower as my humble offering to You!" Lakshmi Ammal has told us that, ever since the incident, she was reminded of Bhagavan's words every time she saw a flowering bush!

There are verses (no.70 & 71) in *Devikalottara* (*Collected Works of Sri Bhagavan*) that say, "It is not advisable to pluck even a flower, without good reason." Our Bhagavan's life was an illustration of this all-encompassing compassion which could not tolerate even the pain inflicted upon a single flower!

32. Sarvam Vasudeva Mayam Jagat

Krishna Premi was an Englishman who was fascinated by the Vaishnavaite philosophy. He became a member of the Gowdiya *math*. It was established by Chaitanya Mahaprabhu and has many followers, especially in West Bengal. One of the most important teachings of Sri Chaitanya is that the entire universe is nothing but a manifestation of Lord Vishnu. *Sarvam Vasudeva Mayam Jagat* (the universe is a manifestation of Vasudeva) is the principal tenet of the *Vaishnava* school of thought, and the followers of Sri Chaitanya had implicit belief in this teaching.

Krishna Premi's very appearance made it clear that he was an extraordinary person. He wore a yellow dhoti around his waist and a towel tied like a turban around his head. With the bright Tilak mark on his forehead and the rosary of Tulsi beads on his neck, he radiated a sense of serene, joyful saintliness. He had a beautiful idol of Radhakrishna which he kept in a small glass case in a bag and carried it with him wherever he went. Only when he retired for the night that he removed the bag and laid it down.

Krishna Premi was a close friend of Dilip Kumar Roy of Sri Aurobindo Ashram. It was Dilip Kumar Roy who urged Krishna Premi to go to Tiruvannamalai and have *darshan* of Bhagavan Sri Ramana. Upon arriving at Sri Ramanasramam, Krishna Premi had *darshan* of Bhagavan and took breakfast with Bhagavan and the other devotees. As he expressed a desire to visit all the places of interest in and around the Arunachala Hill, Viswanatha Swami offered to show him around. He took Krishna Premi to Virupaksha cave and other places. As they walked along, Viswanatha Swami related interesting anecdotes connected with each place they visited. Absorbed in these stories, Krishna Premi lost all sense of time. Eventually, they reached Skandasramam. Here, the serene beauty of the surroundings, as well as the aura of Bhagavan's presence which pervades the place, overwhelmed Krishna Premi. He sat down on a rock, closed his eyes and was immersed in meditation. He remained in this state for a long time. Viswanatha Swami knew that Krishna Premi wanted to have lunch with Bhagavan, but now it was getting late. He went close to Krishna Premi and murmured in his ear, "Sir, we have been in Gokulam for a long time. Sri Krishna is now in Brindavan. Shall we proceed to Brindavan to rejoin our Lord?" As soon as he heard the beloved Name of Sri Krishna, Krishna Premi came out of his trance and they hurried back to Ramanasramam just in time to join Bhagavan for lunch in the dining hall. Viswanatha Swami told Bhagavan about the places he had shown Krishna Premi, and how he had roused him from his deep trance by uttering the name of Sri Krishna, the Lord of Brindavan. Bhagavan smiled appreciatively and said, "Good! Good! So, this Ashram is Brindavan, is it? That is a very good description, indeed!"

Later, Krishna Premi had a very enlightening conversation with Bhagavan. He asked Bhagavan, "Is not the precept, *Sarvam Vasudeva Mayam Jagat* the most wonderful teaching of all time? It makes us think of everything in the universe as being a manifestation of the Divine Being, thus helping us to realise the omnipresent nature of God. Is that not wonderful?" Bhagavan smiled at him and said, "Yes. There is no doubt about that! That is one of the basic tenets of the Vaishnava school, and all the great Vaishnava saints have preached it.

But this can be carried a little further. You say, 'I perceive Vasudeva in everything', but have you found out who this 'I' is? Do all the creatures and objects in creation come to you and say, 'I am Vasudeva'? No. You are the one who says so. Everything depends upon your personal perception. That is to say, you are the only independent force and everything else depends upon you. Moreover, when you say, 'Everything is Vasudeva', do you not include yourself? When you are prepared to accept that plants, animals and even inanimate objects are Vasudeva, why can you not think of yourself as Vasudeva? When you learn to perceive the Lord within yourself, you too become Vasudeva. Do you understand? When the seer identifies himself with Vasudeva, the seen automatically becomes Vasudeva, too. This is what Sri Sankaracharya means when he says, *Drishtim Jnanamayeem Krithva* (Seeing through Eyes of Knowledge)

When he heard this wonderful interpretation of the Truth, Krishna Premi's eyes filled with tears of joy and gratitude. He prostrated to Bhagavan with the utmost love and reverence.

33. Look! Here is a Bald Head!

A lady devotee, who used to stay close to the Ashram, was in the habit of visiting the Ashram every day. After a few years, she had to shift to a nearby town. Even after leaving Tiruvannamalai, she continued to visit the Ashram as frequently as she could. On one of her visits, she was accompnied by her four year old son. The little boy was a bright little bundle of mischief. He refused to sit in one place, but kept running here and there. His sparkling eyes roved everywhere, taking in every small detail. He came close to Bhagavan's sofa and stood at the foot of the sofa for a few minutes, studying Bhagavan. It being a full moon day, Bhagavan had his head shaved that morning. The little boy was also bald. Rubbing his hand over his own head, the child told Bhagavan, "This is a bald head." Then he pointed to Bhagavan and said, "That is another bald head!" Bhagavan joined in the game, by pointing out a shaven-headed devotee and saying, "See! There is another bald head!" At that moment, another devotee entered and the child shouted, "There is another one!" It is the common practice among sadhus to shave their heads on the full moon day. So, there was no shortage of bald heads in the Ashram that day! Bhagavan and the little boy had a grand time, therefore, gleefully pointing out bald heads to each other, and chuckling merrily together! Who but a truly great soul can play such games with a child, without embarrassment or self- consciousness!

* * *

Bhagavan was all praise for the child's boundless energy and power of observation. He then began telling us about some of the remarkable things young visitors had done. Bhagavan said, "Sometimes, children do the most astonishing things.

Sometime back, a little girl used to visit the Ashram regularly with her mother. They stayed nearby in Ramana Nagar and so, the child's mother was able to bring her to the Ashram every afternoon. The little girl would come and sit in the Hall with her mother and observe everything that went on. In those days, some of the visitors would bring some sweets or other snacks to the Ashram. They would place the eatables before me and I would take a little. Then the rest of it would be distributed to all the people in the Hall. The child must have noted this practice. Do you know what she did?"

"It is a common practice among us to roast a few appalams (papads) over the fire and eat it with rice. One day, a few papads had been roasted and kept ready for dinner-time in the child's house. She entered the kitchen and saw the papads. Immediately, she was reminded of the practice of taking eatables to Ramanasramam. She took two of the papads, hid them under her blouse, and hurried to the Ashram. On entering the Hall, she was overcome by shyness and just stood silently in the doorway. I noticed her and called her to my side. She came and stood before me, but still did not say a word. I asked her, "Have you come all alone?" She nodded her head. Then I said, "Why did you come alone? Does your mother know that you are here?" She did not reply. I noticed that her hand was inside her blouse and asked, "What are you holding in your hand? Let me see! Is it something for me?" The child nodded her head and held out her papads to me with a shy smile. I broke off a piece from one of the papads and gave her the rest, saying, "I have taken a little. This is your share." The little girl was overjoyed. She was full of pride at the way she had acted... just like a grown-up!

This is the way with young children. They watch the things adults do, and they want to copy all the actions of their elders.

On another occasion, the same little girl brought me a ripe
guava from their garden. This time also, she had come alone. I
knew that the child was acting on her own. I did not want her
to continue bringing eatables to Bhagavan without her parents'
knowledge. At the same time, I did not want to hurt her tender
feelings. So I said to her, "Do you have a picture of Bhagavan
in your house?" She said, "yes". "Then you can do one thing," I
told her, "Every time you feel like giving something to Bhagavan,
place it before the picture and say, 'Bhagavan, this is for you'.
That is enough. If you offer it to the picture of Bhagavan in
your house, it is the same as offering it to Bhagavan in the Hall.
You need not come all the way to the Ashram every time. Do
you understand?" The child nodded wisely and returned home
with her 'share' of the guava. She must have understood my
words, because she did not bring me any gifts after that!"

Who but Bhagavan could have dealt so tactfully with the
delicate feelings of a small child!

34. THE PEACOCK AND THE KOLAM (DESIGN)

In every description of an Ashram of the Vedic times,
reference is made to the birds and beasts that wandered fearlessly
on the grounds, mingling freely with the human residents of
the Ashram. We read about deer frolicking, of cuckoos singing,
of peacocks dancing, of monkeys playing on the branches of
fruit laden trees, and of bees humming in the blossoming
creepers. In modern times, is it possible to find such a lovely
setting for an Ashram? Yes, indeed! Ramanasramam is just as
lovely as one of the Ashrams of the Vedic period. Dogs, cats,
monkeys, cows, squirrels, sparrows and other birds, all came to

Bhagavan and immersed themselves in the flood of Love that flowed from Bhagavan. In fact, these innocent creatures enjoyed more privileges than a mere human being could hope for!

On entering the gates of the Ashram, the visitor's attention is drawn to the groups of monkeys and the peacocks with their spectacular feathers. These beautiful birds seemed to know that they were particular favourites of Bhagavan, for they strutted about as though they owned the place! And the monkeys were everywhere! Their pranks were not just tolerated, but were actually appreciated greatly (sometimes even encouraged!) by Bhagavan. The animals seemed to be able to communicate perfectly with Bhagavan. Often Bhagavan would point to some particular monkey and say things like, "He is the newly elected king of his tribe. He has come to tell me about his victory over his old rival. And I see that he has brought his queen to be introduced to me. This is a great honour indeed!"

The cow Lakshmi was another esteemed member of this privileged group of Ramana devotees! No daughter could have enjoyed more privileges in her father's house than this cow in Bhagavan's Ashram.

As for the peacocks, they came and went as they pleased. Many of Bhagavan's devotees believe that Bhagavan is an incarnation of Lord Subrahmanya. The intimacy of the relationship between Bhagavan and the peacocks seems to provide the clinching proof of this belief.

While Bhagavan was in the Jubilee Hall, the peacocks were very happy, because they were able to come and see Bhagavan whenever they felt like it. They could enter the Hall from any direction, and they always had unhindered access to their beloved Bhagavan at all times. The way the peacocks craned their necks to gaze at Bhagavan's sweet face, the way they 'asked' him for snacks, and the concern with which Bhagavan fed them tasty tidbits like cashewnuts, groundnuts and dried fruits...all these cannot be described in words. At times, Bhagavan...the same Bhagavan who never asked for anything for himself...would send someone to the store-room with an urgent demand for different kinds of nuts, just for his feathered friends!

The undisputed king of the Ashram peacocks was the white peacock presented by the Queen of Baroda. The bird was unique, not only because of its colour, but also because it enjoyed several privileges which were not extended to the other peacocks in the Ashram. While all the other peacocks spent the night perched on the branches of trees, the white peacock alone slept in a cage placed close to Bhagavan's sofa. Before the white peacock came to the Ashram, Bhagavan used to spend the nights in the old hall. But after its arrival, Bhagavan moved into the Jubilee Hall, because he did not want the peacock to feel lonely! If the attendants ever said anything about this, Bhagavan invariably replied, "Is it not our duty to take good care of our guests? Would it not be improper to make our guests sleep in the open, while we enjoy the shelter of our comfortable hall?"

The white peacock often came to the hall, apparently looking for its beloved Master. If the Hall happened to be crowded, the peacock would hesitate to enter. At such times, Bhagavan would immediately sense its hesitation, and he would welcome it with a charming smile and an affectionate greeting. Encouraged by Bhagavan's call, the peacock would enter the Hall with confidence, and go directly to Bhagavan's side. Bhagavan would fondle it and feed it with some delicacy like nuts or puffed rice. The peacock would then walk out, satisfied with the meeting!

Mere words are inadequate to express the sweetness of Bhagavan's voice and the loving concern in his compassionate eyes. Those who had been fortunate enough to witness Bhagavan's interaction with birds and animals, can never forget those heart-warming incidents.

On a *Jayanti* day, the Ashram had been beautifully decorated with attractive coloured *kolams* (decorative patterns drawn with rice flour and coloured powders). Just in front of the guesthouse, there was a particularly beautiful kolam. It was the drawing of a peacock, and it was so life-like that everyone remarked on its beauty. Bhagavan admired the kolam on his way to the cowshed. On his way back, Bhagavan noticed one of the Ashram peacocks standing near the guest-room. The peacock was gazing at the kolam with apparent fascination. In fact, the bird was so engrossed in the *kolam* that it even ignored the dried fruits and nuts that a devotee was holding out for it. Bhagavan watched the peacock for a few moments, and then said to it, in tones of affectionate amusement, "What is it, dear? Are you afraid that a new bird has come to take your place? No, no! That is no rival!" Hearing this, the live bird seemed to regain its confidence. It was reassured by Bhagavan's tone of voice, and soon it started pecking at the fruits and nuts that had been offered to it. Then it walked away with its usual proud, confident air.

Bhagavan said to his devotees, "What a wonderfully gifted artist! If this kolam could create so much confusion in the real bird, how realistic it should be! Only an extraordinarily subtle intellect could have created such a realistic piece of art. For someone so gifted, Self-enquiry and realisation would be very easy to attain. But unfortunately, such people do not show much interest in the Quest for Truth. Having drawn a peacock that could arrest the attention of a live peacock, this artist will feel inspired to draw a peacock that would induce a living bird to spread its fan and dance! The urge will always be to attain perfection in the artistic ability, and not to seek the Perfection within!"

Even after coming into the Hall and seating himself on the sofa, Bhagavan continued in the same vein. He said, "Only an artist can fully appreciate the skill of another artist. Take the case of a musician. No amount of praise from mere music lovers can please him so much as the appreciation of a fellow musician.

Sri Sankaracharya had to master all the arts and sciences, before he could ascend the *Sarvajna Peetam* (Throne of Supreme Knowledge). In this connection, he had to learn to make some articles with leather. While Sankara was stitching a pair of leather slippers, he rubbed the needle on the bridge of his nose to moisten it. A cobbler, who was looking on, was astounded by the absolutely natural and un-selfconscious manner in which he did it. Sankaracharya had attained total identification with the role of a cobbler! This is the very essence of artistry. Such absorption and identification of oneself with something is not easy."

35. REALISATION THROUGH MUSIC?

Sri Bhagavan was like the mythical *kalpa vriksha* (wish-fulfilling tree). The devotee's slightest wish, even the unspoken ones, would be fulfilled, by merely coming into Bhagavan's presence.

Once, a lady from Andhra Pradesh had come to the Ashram. She was well versed in music, and played the veena very well. She often visited the Ashram and would sometimes render a few songs, either vocally or on the veena.

This lady had a doubt, and she was waiting for the right opportunity to speak to Bhagavan about it. One morning, when there was not much of a crowd in the Hall, the lady approached

Bhagavan and asked, "Bhagavan, is it possible to attain Moksha (Liberation) through music alone or would other spiritual practices be required?"

Bhagavan did not say anything at all. Unable to interpret Bhagavan's silence, the lady pursued the matter, saying, "Did not Saint Thyagaraja and others gain Moksha through singing the praises of the Lord?"

Bhagavan smiled and said, "Saint Thyagaraja and others did not attain Realisation through the songs that they sang. Rather, their songs are the expression of the ecstasy within, the result of their Realisation of the Ultimate. And that is the reason why their songs have survived the test of time." This is what is called Nadopanishad.

The lady was astonished by the simple yet unambiguous way in which Bhagavan had elucidated this great truth. She prostrated to Bhagavan and said, "Your words have cleared all my doubts, Bhagavan! I realise now, that I had been fooling myself all these days, with my half-baked ideas and mistaken beliefs. Bhagavan's grace has opened my eyes and shown me the truth. Now my mind is clear and free."

36. SRI MURUGANAR

Muruganar's devotion for Bhagavan was so strong that he acquired the nickname 'Bhagavan's Shadow'. He has composed innumerable poems in praise of Bhagavan's infinite Grace and Power. Muruganar's poetry is notable, not only for its beauty of expression, but also for the depth of feeling.

Muruganar was born in August 1890 in Ramanathapuram district of Tamil Nadu. His father was Krishna Iyer and his mother was Subbulakshmi Ammal. He had a sister named Kamakshi. Krishna Iyer passed away when his son was just a young boy. Muruganar's actual name was Subrahmanian. He was called Sambamoorthy at home. For the first five years of his life, the child did not utter a single word. Maybe he was saving all his speech to be poured forth in a torrent of exquisite poetry in his later life!

Muruganar attended the Christian Mission School in Ramanathapuram. After passing the X Std., he went to Madurai and stayed with a relative for two years, completed his Matriculation and returned home. Upon his return to Ramanathapuram, Muruganar was approached by one Veluswami Thevar, a member of the royal family, with a request to teach him the *Tirukkural*. The entire family had a deep love for the Tamil language. When they came to know about Muruganar's ability as a teacher, many members of the family approached him for the clarification of their doubts. As a result of his association with them, Muruganar gained the respect and the good wishes of the royal family.

At that time, the renowned Tamil scholar, Raosahib Mu.Raghava Iyengar, was the court poet of the Royal Court of Ramanathapuram. There was another great poet in the same court and, by a strange coincidence, he was also called Raghava Iyengar! With the patronage of the royal family, these two poets made a significant contribution to Tamil Literature. Thanks to his association with the royal family; Muruganar had the opportunity to work with these great scholars.

Muruganar joined some other scholars in making a critical study of the five great Tamil Classics, namely, *Silappadhikaram*, *Manimekalai*, *Seevakachintamani*, *Valaiyapathi* and *Kundalakesi*. This was followed by research into other Tamil literary works like *Tirukkural*, *Nannool* and *Naishadam*. Muruganar had a specially remarkable understanding of Tiruvalluvar's immortal work, *Tirukkural.*

Several of the Tamil scholars of the day had joined to compile a Tamil Dictionary. Muruganar was one of the members of the Committee. As a result of his involvement in this project, Muruganar had the opportunity to work closely with great scholars like Raosahib Mu.Raghava Iyengar, Mahamahopadhyaya Dr.U.V.Swaminatha Iyer, Rao Bahadur V.S. Sengalvaraya Pillai and Sri Sachidanandam Pillai, etc. All these scholars had a great regard for Muruganar. It was this group of scholars* that wrote the Special Preface for Muruganar's book, *Sri Ramana Sannidhi Murai.*

Rao sahib Raghava Iyengar had a special affection and regard for Muruganar. It was he who persuaded Muruganar to take up the job of Tamil Teacher in the Norwick High School for Girls, in Madras. While he was working in Madras, Muruganar's wife, Meenakshi, and his mother were staying with him. Muruganar's father-in-law, Dandapani Swami, was a devotee of Bhagavan. On one of his visits to Madras, Dandapani Swami gave Bhagavan's *Arunachala Sthuti Panchakam* and *Who Am I?* to his son-in-law and asked him to read the books. Muruganar was captivated by these two books, which are treasure-houses of devotion and philosophy. Upon reading the books, Muruganar developed the desire to go to Tiruvannamalai and have *darshan* of Sri Ramana Maharshi; but the pressures of work made it impossible for him to go at once.

During the mid-term holidays (in September), Muruganar was determined to make a visit to Ramanasramam. With God's Grace, he was able to put his plans into action immediately, and

---

* Sri Bhagavan once showed a group photo of these scholars to the devotees in the hall and pointed out, 'This is our Muruganar!'

he reached Tiruvannamalai on the 21st of September, 1923. Upon reaching Tiruvannamalai, Muruganar saw the tall towers of the Arunachala Temple and went in. He stood in front of the shrine of Lord Arunachaleswara and His Divine Consort, lost in adoration. It was an extremely thrilling experience for him. His excitement reached an even higher pitch when he thought of the visit to Ramanasramam. He suddenly realised that he had not brought any offerings to lay at the Maharshi's feet. Immediately, he sat down and wrote a decad of verses in praise of Bhagavan. This poem, titled *Desika Patikam*, was to be Sri Muruganar's first offering to his Master. With his offering, Muruganar hastened to Ramanasramam and was soon standing in front of Bhagavan, drinking in his form with brimming eyes and a heart overflowing with joy. Bhagavan showered his Grace upon this unique devotee in his own way — with a silent yet eloquent gaze.

That evening, Muruganar joined the others for dinner. After dinner, all the devotees were sitting in Bhagavan's presence. Muruganar suddenly got up, prostrated to Bhagavan and rushed out. Seeing that Muruganar appeared greatly agitated, Bhagavan signalled to Kunjuswami and Arunachala Swami to follow Muruganar. Soon, Muruganar and the two others were on the bank of the Agni *Tirtham*. Muruganar did not seem to have any intentions of slackening his speed. Kunjuswami approached the hurrying form in front of him and gently suggested, "Sir, the moon is shining brightly and the night is cool and beautiful. Why don't we sit on these steps and relax for a while?" Muruganar responded to this suggestion and sat down on the steps with his two new friends. At first, he was silent, but soon he started talking about the strange experience that made him rush out of the Ashram. He said that he had suddenly felt an overpowering excitement that was frightening in its intensity, and that this sudden rush of emotion was too much for him to handle and so he had decided to return home immediately.

To calm him and to reassure him, they started talking about Bhagavan's infinite compassion, the concern and kindness he showered on his devotees, as also the all-encompassing love that Bhagavan gave to every creature, animal and human alike. Gradually, Muruganar calmed down, went back to the Ashram with his friends and stayed for two days. After that, he often came to Tiruvannamalai and stayed in the Ashram for two or three days each time.

Ever since his first *darshan* of Bhagavan, Muruganar was totally won over by him and he lost interest in everything else.

Muruganar was a staunch Gandhian and wore only *khadi* garments. As he believed in the principle of *Ahimsa* (non-violence) he would not travel in vehicles drawn by horses or bulls. He therefore walked to the Ashram, all the way from the Railway Station in Tiruvannamalai Town.

Muruganar was totally captivated by Bhagavan, and could not stay away from Bhagavan and Ramanasramam for long. Every time he felt the urge to see Bhagavan, he would immediately catch the train and come to the Ashram. When it was time to return to Madras, he just could not bear to leave Bhagavan. He would somehow force himself to leave the Ashram and would set off for the Railway Station. But in a short while, he would be back in the Ashram! With his characterestic perception, Bhagavan understood Muruganar's difficulty, and arranged for someone to go with Muruganar, just to make sure he reached the Station! Someone would accompany Muruganar to the Station. Once his companion had left him, however, Muruganar would completely forget the reason for his being in the Railway Station. He would wander up and down the platform, oblivious to all the activity around him. The train would arrive and then leave, amidst the ringing of bells and the blowing of whistles. Muruganar would not notice all the noise and the bustle, but would continue walking up and down, lost in thoughts of Sri Bhagavan. Long after the train had left, Muruganar would suddenly emerge from his reverie. He would look around in obvious confusion and after a few minutes, would make his way back to the Ashram.

Upon his return to the Ashram, Bhagavan would ask Muruganar, "Didn't the train come on time?" When he heard that the train had arrived on time, Bhagavan would ask, "Then why did you not board the train?" In a dazed tone of voice, Muruganar would reply, "I just didn't feel like getting into the train, Bhagavan!" The next time Muruganar made preparations for going to Madras, Bhagavan would make it a point to send someone with him, to see that Muruganar actually boarded the train!

In this fashion, Muruganar carried on with his life, travelling between Madras and Tiruvannamalai at frequent intervals. He wanted to wind up the household in Madras and settle down in Tiruvannamalai, but circumstances were not favourable. His mother was old and infirm, and Muruganar had to stay in Madras for her sake.

In three years' time, Muruganar's mother passed away. He performed the last rites as prescribed. He took his mother's ashes to Dhanushkoti and dissolved a major portion of it in the sea there. Then, with the balance of his mother's ashes in an urn, Muruganar came to Tiruvannamalai. He placed the urn at the foot of a tree, had his bath, and went into the hall. When Bhagavan saw Muruganar, he enquired with touching concern, "Were you able to complete the last rites for your mother, without any trouble?" Bhagavan's gentle tone and compassionate words shattered Muruganar's composure, and he broke down completely. Kunju Swami, who was nearby, said to Bhagavan, "Muruganar has brought his mother's ashes in an urn." Bhagavan said, "That is good. The Agni *Tirtham* is a suitable spot for dissolving the ashes." Muruganar took Bhagavan's advice and dissolved the ashes in the Agni *Tirtham*.

After his mother's passing away, Muruganar resigned his job in Madras, wound up the household there, and came to Tiruvannamalai for good in 1926. At first, he stayed in the Palakothu. He lived on alms, going into the town to beg every morning. On several occasions, he went without food for the entire day, because he had missed the trip into town. Bhagavan used to say that, by begging for one's food, one can easily conquer the ego. Muruganar's faith in this principle was very strong. Every morning, he would set off on his rounds, with a white towel in which he collected the food he received as alms. Then he would come to Palakothu, lay the bundle of food on the bank of the pond, and wade into the water to clean his hands and feet. Muruganar was very fastidious, when it came to personal hygiene. He would scrub his hands and legs with mud several times, till he was satisfied that they were quite clean. Naturally, this took a lot of time. The monkeys in the area would come and devour all the food that Muruganar had collected. Finally when he came out of the water, he would find that all his food was gone. He had no choice but to go without food that day.

Sabhapathi Pillai, who was in charge of the Vinayaka Temple in Palakothu, once saw the monkeys plundering Muruganar's food. Out of concern for the hapless Muruganar, Sabhapathi Pillai offered to stay within the temple premises, and asked Muruganar to stay in his room. During the time of Muruganar's stay in Palakothu, Kunju Swami, Munagala Venkatrama Iyer, Visvanatha Swami, Ramanatha Brahmachari and Ramasubba Iyer were also staying there. All of them being Bhagavan's staunch devotees, they enjoyed each other's company greatly. Kunju Swami often spoke of those days with a lot of nostalgic feeling.

Of all Bhagvan's devotees, Muruganar and Pudukkottai K. Lakshmana Sarma were privileged to learn the scriptures directly from Bhagavan.

Natesa Swami, the Head of the Esanya *math*, had heard about Muruganar's capabilities as a teacher. He therefore requested Muruganar to stay in the *Math* and teach him Manickavachakar's *Tiruchitrambala Kovai*. Accordingly, Muruganar went to stay in the Esanya *math*. Every morning, he would take class for Natesa Swami and, in the afternoon, he would come to Ramanasramam.

In those days, Sadhu Natanaananda was staying in the Guhai Namasivaya *math* on the Arunachala Hill. Natanaananda would time his own visit to Ramanasramam in such a way that he would meet Muruganar near the Western Tower of Arunachaleswara Temple, every afternoon. From this spot, both of them would walk to Ramanasramam together. Muruganar used to compose some verses and bring them along every day. During their walk, the two friends would discuss Muruganar's latest composition. One day, it so happened that Muruganar was able to compose only the first four lines of a verse. Try as he might, he could not complete the verse. Natanaananda read the four lines, and wrote another four lines, thus completing the verse.

When they reached the Ashram, they showed the poem to Bhagavan, and told him the story behind it. Bhagavan smiled at Natanaananda and said, " Tomorrow, you should write the first four lines of a poem, and get Muruganar to complete the verse for you." Natanaananda did just that, and the second poem was also shown to Bhagavan. After reading the poem, Bhagavan said, "Good! It looks like we have twin poets here! You should name the first poem 'Muruga Natana' and the second one 'Natana Muruga'!" Everyone present was very much entertained by this amazing incident.

In addition to practising Self-enquiry prescribed by Bhagavan, his devotees also gave a lot of importance to *giripradakshinam*. *Giripradakshinam* is a potent way of attaining Self-Realisation. Muruganar performed *giripradakshinam* for 48 consecutive days. During *pradakshina* between the Nirudhi Lingam and Adi Annamalai, he had no body-consciousness.

From 1923 to 1973, i.e., for half a century, Muruganar has poured forth his love and reverence for Bhagavan in thousands of beautiful poems. *Sri Ramana Sannidhi Murai* contains 1,851 poems in praise of Bhagavan. Every one of the poems in this book is a rare combination of literary perfection and heartfelt emotion.

In addition to *Sri Ramana Sannidhi Murai*, Muruganar has composed *Sri Ramana Devamaalai, Sri Ramana Charana Pallaandu, Sri Ramana Anubhooti, Sri Ramana Alankaram*, and *Sri Ramana Jnanabhodham*. The collection of Bhagavan's teachings by Muruganar titled *Guru Vachaka Kovai* has the distinction of being edited by Bhagavan himself. In addition to all this, Muruganar has written a very detailed commentary for Bhagavan's *Aksharamanamalai*.

In the first few months of his stay in Tiruvannamalai, Muruganar resided in Palakothu. Afterwards, in response to the request of Dr.T.N. Krishnaswami Iyer of Madras,

Muruganar came to stay in his building opposite to Ramanasramam. Padma and I were also tenants in the same building. It was while we were all in the same premises that Muruganar started teaching me and Padma the *Nool Tirattu* of Bhagavan and the scriptures. Padma and I did our best to be of assistance to Muruganar.

In 1971, Muruganar was shifted to the room near the Ashram dispensary as his health was deteriorating. The Ashram took up the responsibility of providing for all his needs, like food and medical care. In spite of the best treatment and attention, however, Muruganar's condition worsened and on the 28th of August, 1973, Muruganar left this world. His mortal remains have been enshrined at the foot of the Hill, within the Ashram premises. Every year, devotees perform special *puja* in memory of this great devotee of Bhagavan. Now let us read some more incidents connected with Muruganar.

37. THE MASTER WHO DEVOURS EVERYTHING

One of the advantages we enjoyed was that we could benefit from Bhagavan's conversations with various people. Someone or the other would ask a question. Bhagavan's answers were always short and to the point. Yet, Bhagavan's words seemed to be addressed directly and personally to every member in the gathering. Sometimes, a devotee would have a doubt or a problem which he was reluctant to discuss in the presence of strangers. In such situations, somebody else would ask Bhagavan a question, and Bhagavan's reply would answer the reticent devotee's unasked question too! This is indeed the greatest miracle of all.

Once, a devotee of Vilakshanananda Swami visited Sri Ramanasramam. He approached Bhagavan and timidly enquired, "Our Guru tells us to repeat the Name of the Lord a fixed number of times every day, and surrender to him the spiritual merit thus acquired. What is the practice here?" Bhagavan laughed heartily at the cleverness of the Guru who accumulated vast spiritual 'wealth' without having to work for it! When Muruganar entered the hall, Bhagavan beckoned him and said, "Look! Isn't this a marvelous idea? This person's Guru tells all his disciples to do *nama japa* (recitation of the Name) so many times every day, and collects the spiritual merit as his due. I wonder what the disciples get after this surrender! This is like paying out regular instalments of interest on a loan, isn't it? How do you like the idea?"

Muruganar replied, "O Bhagavan! Their Guru is certainly far better than you! He only demands the interest, leaving the principal intact. But 'You' swallow up everything — principal, interest and all! When the individual himself has disappeared, who is there to repay the loan? And anyway, the principal and the interest also get wiped out. Nothing at all remains." As he spoke, Muruganar's eyes filled with tears and his voice was choked with emotion. Bhagavan merely smiled, and remained silent.

What Muruganar meant was that Bhagavan wipes out the mind and the ego of his devotees. Once the mind has disappeared without trace, where is the instrument for doing japa or meditation? The mind is the 'principal' that has been loaned to us for this lifetime, and nama japa is the interest to be paid on this principal. How can one pay the interest when the principal itself has disappeared? The destruction of the principal (the mind/ego) is a matter for rejoicing. When Bhagavan 'confiscates the principal' i.e., when his glance of Grace destroys the mind, the fortunate devotee is forever free of his liabilities. He no longer has to worry about paying 'interest' in the form of japa etc. The destruction of the 'principal', therefore, brings great joy!

38. AVVAIYAR'S POETIC SKILL

Tiruvalluvar was one of the greatest of Tamil poets. In his immortal Tirukkural, he has recorded the wisdom of the ages. The greatness of the Tirukkural lies in the fact that the highest philosophical truths and the most pragmatic advice about everyday life and values, have been presented in pithy verses, each verse being no more than 1$^{3/4}$ lines in length.

Once, Bhagavan's devotees were discussing Tiruvalluvar's skill in condensing the greatest truths into the shortest of verses. Someone mentioned that Idaikkadar, one of the famous poets of the Sangam Age, had composed a verse in praise of Tiruvalluvar's unique ability. Idaikkadar says, "So much wisdom has been condensed into such compact verses that it seems as though Tiruvalluvar has drilled a hole in a single mustard seed and filled it with all the waters of the Seven Seas!"

Bhagavan, who was listening to this discussion, turned to Muruganar and said, "Hasn't Avvaiyar condensed the Kural even further?" To this query, Muruganar replied, "Yes, indeed! Avvaiyar has composed a poem of amazing brevity and unmatched beauty. It is an interesting story. Once, a group of poets were discussing the greatness of Tiruvalluvar and the unique nature of the Tirukkural. Avvaiyar was asked to give her opinion. She said, "All of you seem to be highly impressed by the so-called brevity of the Tirukkural. But is it really so very concise and compact? Can a collection of 1330 couplets, divided into 133 chapters, be thought of as being 'brief' or 'concise'? I cannot see the need for so many verses, just to tell us about Virtue, Wealth and Happiness. In my opinion, the Tirukkural is an unnecessarily long composition."

The other poets were taken aback by Avvaiyar's words. They did not believe that the matter in the Tirukkural could possibly be condensed any further. So they challenged Avvaiyar to compose a really short poem which could be considered equal to the Tirukkural in brevity, clarity and beauty. Immediately, Avvaiyar responded with the following poem:

"Charity is the supreme virtue; wealth is that which is earned through lawful means; the happiness that is enjoyed by a loving couple through the union of minds is the only true happiness. The renunciation of Virtue, Wealth and Happiness, in order to seek the Supreme, results in Everlasting Bliss."

Muruganar said, "Whereas Valluvar had dealt with the three subjects of Virtue, Wealth and Happiness, Avvaiyar had included Realisation also in her four-line poem.* All the other poets were speechless with wonder!" Bhagavan and his devotees, too, were full of appreciation for Avvaiyar's unique skill as a poet.

This anecdote is certainly not known to many. It is doubtful whether even a scholar specialising in ancient Tamil literature would have heard about it. But to a devotee of Bhagavan, such precious pearls of wisdom are easy to come by. Such is the power of Bhagavan's presence.

---

x* ஈதல்அறம் தீவினைவிட்டு ஈட்டல் பொருள்
காதல் இருவர் கருத்துஒருமித்து - ஆதரவு
பட்டதே இன்பம் பரனைநினைந்து இம்மூன்றும்
விட்டதே பேரின்ப வீடு.

39. Avial and Adiammal

Bhagavan was particular that no visitor to the Ashram should go away hungry. At meal times, be it breakfast, lunch or dinner, Bhagavan always insisted that everybody should take food. If, for some reason, someone happened to miss a meal, Bhagavan used to feel bad about it. If he noticed that someone was absent at meal time, he would personally check up on that person and see to it that he had something to eat. Adiammal was a lady from Nellore, who had great devotion for Bhagavan. She was a frequent visitor to the Ashram, and often made liberal donations towards its upkeep. This lady was a close friend of Varanasi Subbulakshmi Ammal, who was an assistant in the Ashram kitchen.

Adiammal was on one of her visits to the Ashram. In the dining hall, she found herself almost directly opposite to Bhagavan's place. Bhagavan entered the hall and seated himself in his usual place. The attendants started serving the food. When everybody had been served, Bhagavan usually nodded his head as a signal for everyone to start. That particular day, when Bhagavan glanced around the hall, he saw Adiammal standing in front of her leaf-plate. He gestured to her to sit down, saying, "Why are you standing? Please sit down and begin your meal." At once, Adiammal sat down.

Adiammal was elated because Bhagavan had addressed her personally. The next day also, she remained standing until Bhagavan noticed her and told her to sit down. The third day, Adiammal again stood in front of her leaf plate, waiting for Bhagavan to notice her. She was hoping that he would address her personally, as on the previous occasions. But this time, Bhagavan did not say anything at all. Adiammal continued to stand; everybody else was busy eating. That day, some festival was being celebrated and so, *avial* (a special South Indian dish containing a variety of vegetables with curd) had been prepared. While serving the *avial* on Bhagavan's leaf, Shantamma said in a low voice, "Bhagavan, Adiammal is still standing. Will not Bhagavan ask her to sit down?" Bhagavan responded to this, saying, "Oh! There is a Subbulakshmi Ammal to take care of Adiammal. But what about Muruganar? Who is there to take care of him? See, you have prepared Avial today. Has anyone thought of giving a portion of this special dish to Muruganar?"

Shanthammal was deeply touched by Bhagavan's loving concern for Muruganar. She said, "I will go right away, and give Muruganar some of this Avial." She hurried into the kitchen, scooped up some Avial in a coconut shell, and set off to Palakothu in search of Muruganar. By the time Shanthammal left the Ashram with the *avial* in her hand, Muruganar had left Palakothu and started out to ask for alms. He had just reached the Dakshinamoorthy temple (opposite the Mourvi Guest House) when Shanthammal saw him. She hurried after him, calling, "Sambamoorthy! Sambamoorthy!" (Shanthammal and Muruganar had been neighbours in their childhood and so she always called him 'Sambamoorthy', which was his childhood name.) On hearing Shanthammal's voice, Muruganar looked around and, seeing her hurrying towards him, he stood still and waited for her. By the time she reached him, poor Shanthammal was out of breath. She gasped, "A fine person you are, wandering around like a madman, while Bhagavan is so concerned about you! Why don't you come to the Ashram and have your meals with the rest of the devotees?" She proceeded to relate the details of the incident in the dining hall.

Muruganar was stunned. He was overcome by emotion when he heard about Bhagavan's concern for his welfare. He kept repeating, "Did Bhagavan say that? Was he worried about me? Did he say, 'Who will take care of Muruganar?' Such concern for me! How fortunate I am!" His voice grew hoarse and his eyes filled with tears; his face was flushed with emotion. Unable to support his frame, he simply sat on the steps of the temple. He raised the coconut shell to his eyes and reverently poured the Avial into his cupped palms and ate it as Bhagavan's sacred *Maha prasad.* He decided not to proceed with his *biksha* that day. His heart was so full that it mattered little that his stomach was far from full! Bhagavan's love and concern for Muruganar, was wonderful indeed!

40. RAMANAANTHAM

Once, a scholar from the Kovilur *math* came to see Muruganar. He had a good knowledge of both the scriptures and the literary works in Tamil. He had heard about Muruganar's poetic genius, and had come to Tiruvannamalai especially to meet him. Muruganar had stayed in the Kovilur *math* for some time, and he knew the head of the *math* quite well. Muruganar and the head of the Kovilur *math* had a lot of regard for each other. So, upon the scholar's arrival at Ramanasramam, Muruganar spent some time making enquiries about his old acquaintances in the *math.* After a while, the conversation changed to literary and philosophical works. The visitor wanted to know about Bhagavan's teachings — both the written works and the answers to the questions posed by devotees. Muruganar gave him the information he sought and the visitor was amazed at the efficacy and the freshness of Bhagavan's teachings. Soon afterwards, the visitor left on a *giripradakshinam.* He returned to the Ashram in the afternoon.

At that time, Muruganar was explaining to me *Ozhivil Odukkam*. The visitor from the Kovilur *math* sat with us and listened attentively to Sri Muruganar's words. The written commentary to the *Ozhivil Odukkam* was based on the philosophical interpretations of the work. Muruganar would explain the *Collected Works* of Bhagavan. Then he would illustrate the same point by telling me about some incident or remark made by Bhagavan.

At the end of the lesson, the visitor asked Muruganar, "Sir, please tell me one thing. Are your explanations based on *Siddhanta* or *Vedanta*?"

Muruganar was rather surprised by this question. Obviously, he had never considered the matter. After a few moments of thought, he said, "I know neither *Siddhanta* nor *Vedanta*. All I know is Bhagavan and the Truth as he has taught it to me. So, maybe the best description for my interpretation would be "*Ramanaantham*." The visitor could see that Muruganar was in a highly emotional state. So he refrained from asking any further questions.

Normally commentaries are classified into *Vedanta-param* and *Siddhanta-param*. Bhagavan based his teachings on his own experience of the Truth and needed no corroboration from either the scriptural or the philosophical texts. Bhagavan's emphasis on Self-enquiry can be considered a revolutionary approach to the search for the Eternal Truth.

If Bhagavan is to be considered a revolutionary teacher, Muruganar certainly deserves to be known as a revolutionary disciple. Who but an exceptional disciple could have coined the term *Ramanaantham* to describe Ramana's Way!

Sadguru Thyagaraja's musical compositions are known to the music world as *Thyagopanishad* (the *Upanishad* of

Thyagaraja). In the same way, Bhagavan's devotees revere their Master's teachings as *Ramanopanishad* or *Ramanaantham*.

41. SARASWATI PUJA

The Navaratri festival is celebrated at the Matrubhuteswara Temple at Ramanasramam. This festival is dedicated to the Mother Goddess in Her various manifestations. It is a nine-day festival, and the ninth day is celebrated as Saraswati *puja* or the worship of Goddess Saraswati. On this day, the traditional practice is to offer worship to books.

True to tradition, some books had been arranged on a stool placed beside Bhagavan's sofa. Muruganar entered the hall and seeing the pile of books with flowers strewn over them, was quite amused. He gave Bhagavan an eloquent look and received an enigmatic smile in reply. No words were required; the communication between them was perfect and total.

Muruganar could not understand the need for any symbols of divinity, when God Himself was seated in the hall. That is why the worship of books in Bhagavan's presence struck him as being superfluous. In lines 321 and 322 of the *Ramana Puranam*, Muruganar says, "All ancient texts and their expositions put together can be no more than a preface to the Book of your Powerful Silence!" He was amused by the idea of worshipping a pile of books in the very presence of the Repository of all Knowledge, Bhagavan Sri Ramana Maharshi! Muruganar expressed his feelings in the form of a very beautiful poem, which he wrote on a piece of paper and handed to Bhagavan:

"Bhagavan! This idea of placing books beside your sofa and worshipping them with due reverence, is like placing the chaff of sugarcane beside sugarcandy. You are the sweet personification of perfection, O Bhagavan! These books are like the crushed sugarcane from which all the juice has been extracted. Of what value is the crushed sugarcane waste when one has the beautiful sugar-figurine in one's possession? You are the personification of the essence of all the knowledge contained in all the scriptures. When you are here with us, can these books have any real value?

Maybe these books deserve to be worshipped, after all. It could be that the crushed sugarcane considers itself worthy of respect because it is in the sugarcane that the sugar-idol originated. It seems to me that the sugarcane might expect some recognition for this fact and has asked to be worshipped, for this reason."

Bhagavan read this poem with a smile. At the end, he looked at Muruganar and nodded his head in appreciation of the views expressed in the poem. Muruganar later remarked to some friends that the incident struck him as being as inexplicable as wanting to worship a portrait of Bhagavan in the very presence of Bhagavan himself!

* * *

An incident occured a few days later. A new visitor to the Ashram was telling Bhagavan that he had been worshipping Lord Subrahmanya with great devotion for ten years, but the Lord had not chosen to appear before him. The devotee was obviously in anguish, and might have expected Bhagavan to give him some advice. But Bhagavan merely nodded his head and said, 'Is that so?' Muruganar who was sitting in the hall became emotional and said to the devotee, "Sir! Your prayers have been effective indeed! Look before you! Who is this, in front of your eyes!" The devotee opened his eyes wide and gazed at Bhagavan. Within moments, his eyes filled with tears of ecstasy and he exulted, "Yes! My prayers have been granted! My Subrahmanya is right here! I am fortunate indeed!"

Later in the evening, this devotee went to Muruganar and told him, "Thank you, Sir, for directing me. I looked at Bhagavan and saw Lord Subrahmanya with His two Consorts. Bhagavan Sri Ramana is none other than Lord Subrahmanya!"

Several devotees have reported similar incidents, i.e., seeing Bhagavan as the manifestation of their own favourite deities. Muruganar, for his part, sang the glory of Sri Bhagavan as the manifestation of all the gods.

42. THE UNSKILLED ARTISAN

In the early days, before Ramanasramam was established, Bhagavan's devotees used to enjoy certain privileges, which were denied to them later. For example, it was possible for the devotees to obtain the leaf-plate which Bhagavan had used, and to eat from it themselves, thus getting the satisfaction of enjoying a very intimate relationship with their Master. In those days, Bhagavan used to wash his hands in a basin; devotees vied with each other to obtain this water, which was considered sacred Prasad. Devotees also enjoyed the privilege of collecting the water with which Bhagavan had washed his feet, and sprinkling it on their own heads as a benediction.

Bhagavan never encouraged such practices. The devotees were able to indulge in such activities because Bhagavan was unaware of what was going on. When the devotees started doing all this blatantly, and especially when they started competing with each other for these 'privileges', Bhagavan firmly put a stop to such practices.

There was a secret agreement among the Ashram attendants, according to which they took turns, eating from the leaf-plate Bhagavan had used during lunch and dinner. These arrangements were kept a closely guarded secret. Somehow, Muruganar came to know that such a thing was going on, and he developed the desire to enjoy this rare privilege at least once. Accordingly, Muruganar entered the dining hall one day, after Bhagavan had finished his lunch. He was hesitating at the entrance, wondering whom to approach and how to obtain Bhagavan's leaf-plate, when he saw Shanthammal in the dining hall. Muruganar and Shanthammal were from the same town Ramanathapuram, and had known each other from childhood. So Muruganar thought that his task would become easy. On hearing Muruganar's wish, Shanthammal told him that, in the day-time, it was only the attendants who took away Bhagavan's leaf, and that Muruganar would have to wait till dinner time for a chance to obtain Bhagavan's leaf-plate.(Mudaliar grandma used to send food at lunch time for Bhagavan. As he belonged to a higher caste, Shanthammal thought that Muruganar was not supposed to take the leaf-plate used during lunch.)

Muruganar was badly disappointed. Usually, he never nurtured a desire for anything. His one desire of obtaining Bhagavan's leaf-plate, had proved futile. So he poured forth his feelings in the form of a verse: "Lord Brahma, the Creator of the Universe, is very good at chanting all the four *Vedas*; but when it comes to fashioning suitable dwellings for all the souls entering the world, He is obviously incompetent. Let us consider my case. I have the body of a man. Maybe, my actions in previous lives had entitled me to a human body. But the soul that resides in this body is undoubtedly that of a dog. That is why I have developed the desire to eat from your used plate,

O Noble Ramana! I prostrate myself at your feet and beg you
to grant me Real Knowledge."

43. BHAGAVAN AND THE POET

There was an intimacy in the relationship between Muruganar
and Bhagavan which was not obvious at first glance. Theirs was a
relationship that did not require physical closeness. It was a union
of mind and soul, far more intimate than words can describe.
Muruganar's fidelity and single-minded devotion to Bhagavan was
so strong that, once he had started singing in praise of Bhagavan,
he refused to sing about any other God. He considered Bhagavan
the only God, and worshipped him alone. In his *Puranthozha Pathu*,
he says, "Ramana, my Lord! You are a Teacher greater than any
divine Guru, and I will never feel the need to visit any other temple
or worship any other God." He has also categorically stated, "I
shall never worship at any shrine other than that of my Ramana."

Muruganar was one of the greatest Tamil poets of this
century. In fact, Thanigaimani Sengalvaraaya Pillai said that
Muruganar is to be considered an equal to any of the Tamil
poets of the Sangam Era (the period, a few thousand years ago,
which is acknowledged as the Golden Age of Tamil poetry.)
Sengalvaraaya Pillai has written a truly wonderful Introduction
to Muruganar's magnum opus, the *Sri Ramana Sannidhi Murai*.
Mahamahopadhyaya U.V. Swaminatha Iyer has written a special
Preface to this same work.

Muruganar's extraordinary poetic gifts became apparent
while he was still very young. After his meeting with Bhagavan,
his entire personality underwent a change. Not only did the
pattern of his external life change; his spiritual awakening is

also to be attributed to his meeting with Bhagavan. His poetry also acquired a new depth and poignancy after he came under Bhagavan's influence. Once he started singing Bhagavan's praises, Muruganar continued doing so for the rest of his life, dedicating poem after poem to his beloved Master. Every thought and every nuance of feeling was recorded in immortal poetry, and laid at Bhagavan's feet, with the reverence of a devotee laying a wreath of flowers at the altar of his deity. The Alwars and the Nayanmars of olden days have sung many songs glorifying the Feet of the Lord. In the same vein, Muruganar has composed the *Sri Ramana Charana Pallaandu* in praise of Bhagavan's feet, which provide refuge and solace to all true devotees. The *Ramana Sannidhi Murai* begins with the phrase, *Namo Ramanaaya* which is a potent mantra containing six syllables. The *mantra* for Lord Subrahmanya also consists of six syllables. This can be taken as corroboration of the theory that Bhagavan is an incarnation of Lord Subrahmanya.

Muruganar believed that Bhagavan is the only God and that the devotee of Bhagavan need not go in search of any other deity. Once, a group of people made preparations for a pilgrimage. They came to Muruganar and asked him whether he would be interested in joining them. Muruganar replied, "The moment I set eyes on Bhagavan, who is the Sun of Self-Awareness, my eyes became blinded by the brilliance of his Form. Now, I cannot see anything or anybody other than my Bhagavan. This being the case, of what use would a pilgrimage be, for me?"

In his *Sri Ramana Sannidhimurai*, Muruganar has sung about Bhagavan in various different moods, extolling various facets of Bhagavan's greatness, and of his own relationship with Bhagavan. Once he had come into Bhagavan's fold, Muruganar had no worldly ambitions or desires left; everything had been surrendered to Bhagavan. However, Muruganar's love for Tamil and poetry refused to leave him! Muruganar himself ruefully acknowledges this, in one verse: 'O greatest of Saints! I have surrendered my all to you. I have given up my desire for material possessions, for name, fame and family ties; but I have not been able to give up my love for Tamil poetry. This, I admit, is a major flaw. However, I will attain peace by dedicating my poetry to the service of your Lotus Feet.' (v.1226)

After coming to Bhagavan, Muruganar's fascination for *Tirukkural* also started fading. What had been almost an obsession now became a much milder admiration, and Muruganar felt relieved at the softening of his emotions. He expresses this relief in a verse, in which he thanks Bhagavan for freeing him from the spell the *Tirukkural* and other literary works had cast upon him.

In another poem, Muruganar says, "This peerless Brahmin (Ramana), who was born in Tiruchuzhi, has the power to change the destiny of his devotee. Though he himself had no formal instruction in the scriptures, his wisdom and knowledge are of such magnitude as to fill the most learned scholars with admiration. He shines as the Sun of Self- Knowledge, bathing the world in the light of his Grace."

Sri Bhagavan attained Self-realisation at a very young age, without any austerities. Muruganar says, in one of his poems, "Having obtained Self-realisation at a young age, without having to take instructions from others, or even having to make any conscious efforts, you are now bestowing the gift of Self Knowledge upon your devotees through the power of your Presence alone. Your devotees are fortunate indeed, for they are granted the highest of Wisdom without having to undergo the rigours of spiritual exercises."

It is common belief that *yogis* take birth in this world only to finish the process of spiritual evolution which had been left incomplete in previous lives. In one of Muruganar's poems (v.1524 - *Tiruchazhal*), a lady asks her friend, "If not to make up for the deficits of previous lives, why has this Venkataraman come down to earth now? Why else would he be walking about on this earth now?" To this, her friend replies, "Though it may appear as though Venkataraman (Bhagavan Ramana) is leading a mortal's life, the truth of the matter is that he is walking around on this earth barefooted, only to satisfy the Earth Goddess' long-cherished desire to feel the touch of God's Feet." Though God has come down to the Earth in various incarnations, in each of these incarnations He has had various vehicles and His Feet seldom touched the ground directly. So the Earth Goddess felt deprived of the privilege of touching the Divine Feet, and was longing for a chance to do so. In response to Her desire, God came into the world in the form of Sri Ramana and walked barefoot over every inch of the Arunachala Hill, just to please the Goddess Earth. All of us know that Bhagavan never wore any footwear. But Muruganar alone could have come up with such a beautifully moving explanation for Bhagavan's actions!

Lord Siva assumes human form to sport with His devotees. On one occasion, the Lord caused a terrible flood to wash away the banks of the River Vaigai. The Pandya King, faced with the task of rebuilding the banks made it mandatory for each family to send one representative, to help in the building the banks. A devout old lady, Vanthi by name, found herself in a difficult position, because she had nobody to send. Lord Siva, in the form of a handsome youth, now appeared before Vanthi and offered to go to work for her sake. As payment for the work, He demanded that Vanthi should give Him the *pittu* (a South

Indian delicacy made with rice, coconut and jaggery) that she was preparing. Though she had given Him everything she had, Vanthi must have regretted the fact that she could give only pittu to the Lord, and must have longed for a chance to feed Him with a variety of tasty dishes. It is this longing that resulted in Vanthi appearing as seven ladies and lovingly plying Ramana with a variety of dishes, in the course of his walk through the forests around Arunachala Hill. This captivating idea finds expression in one of Muruganar's lovely poems (v.1651 - *Tiruppoovalli*). The poem refers to an incident in Bhagavan's life; a detailed description of this incident can be found in Bhagavan's biography.

Bhagavan had the power of bestowing Self-Knowledge on devotees, through a mere glance of Grace. Muruganar has devoted an entire chapter, *Tirukkannokkam*, to the description of this unique aspect of Bhagavan's Grace. One of the verses (v.1613) in this chapter says: "Due to his constant absorption in the Self, Sri Ramana is always in a state beyond sleep. Therefore, his eyes are always wide open, like the unblinking eyes of a fish swimming in a pool of clear water. If we are fortunate enough to encounter the unblinking gaze of Ramana, my friends, we can obtain all that we wish for!"

There is a beautiful song (v.1507) in the section titled *Tiruvammaanai* which says: "A lady is asked, 'Venkataramanan never bothers to address any words of welcome to those who come to see him. Yet, hordes of devotees rush to him every day, with so much love and enthusiasm. Why should this be so, can you say?' To her friend's question, the lady replies, 'The reason why multitudes of people flock to Sri Ramana with so much enthusiasm and joy is that there is an Ocean of Bliss flowing in front of the flower-soft feet of Ramana, and devotees are eager to immerse themselves in this ocean of joy'."

Bhagavan never asked anybody to come to him; likewise, if someone wanted to leave the Ashram, Bhagavan did not press them to stay on. At times, devotees would come to Bhagavan and tell him about the spiritual exercises that they were pursuing, or the books they were reading, or the method of meditation they were following. Bhagavan merely listened to all this, but never offered any criticism or encouragement. The most he ever said was, 'Is that so? That itself is enough!" In spite of the fact that Bhagavan seldom uttered any words of instruction, devotees flocked to him because, in his holy presence, they found a peace and joy they could find nowhere else.

It is to Muruganar that we owe the priceless gems of Bhagavan's spiritual teachings especially *Upadesa Undiar* and *Ulladu Narpadu*. With Muruganar's repeated requests and untiring persuasion, Bhagavan recorded his teachings in these titles. They contain the very essence of the Vedas. (*Guru Vachaka Kovai — The Garland of Guru's Sayings* by Muruganar is also a collection of Sri Bhagavan's Teachings).

Muruganar attained great bliss through his association with Bhagavan. He acknowledges his debt to Bhagavan in one of the verses in *Ramananubhuti* (v.33): "I am like a bee feeding on the nectar flowing at the feet of Bhagavan Ramana whose Silence is the essence of the teaching that leads to the Realisation of the All-pervading Power of Lord Siva Himself. It is because I am with Sri Ramana that my body, my life, and all my senses are constantly immersed in a state of supreme bliss." Muruganar's *Ramananubhuti* is a work full of praise for Bhagavan Ramana as a teacher, and of Muruganar's gratitude for Bhagavan's Grace.

44. Muruga–Mayavan

Muruganar's devotion for Bhagavan was beyond measure. All his love and devotion for Bhagavan found expression in the beautiful poems he composed in praise of Bhagavan. These poems had a sweetness and a depth of feeling that could not fail to melt the heart of listeners. Bhagavan's devotees used to sing some of Muruganar's poems in the hall, so that everybody could enjoy the beauty of these captivating verses.

Muruganar's wife, Meenakshi Ammal, was also a frequent visitor to the Ashram. Bhagavan was always specially kind and considerate to this lady, and treated her as a favoured guest. Knowing that Meenakshi Ammal loved good coffee, Bhagavan would tell the Ashram cooks, "Give Meenakshi good, strong coffee, just the way she likes it." Bhagavan would also listen patiently to Meenakshi Ammal's complaints about her husband, the chief among those being, of course, that Muruganar was neglecting her and all his domestic responsibilities. On one of her visits, Meenakshi Ammal seemed particularly upset. She told Bhagavan that Muruganar's neglect was very difficult for her to bear, and that Muruganar seemed not to realise just how badly his behaviour was affecting her.

It was Meenakshi Ammal's practice to sing a few verses from Muruganar's Ramana Sannidhi Murai in Bhagavan's presence, everytime she came to the Ashram. On this occasion also, she had a copy of the book with her, and was about to select some suitable chapter. Bhagavan took the book from her hands and, marking the section where there was a decad of verses, each ending with 'Ramana Mayavane', he said to Meenakshi Ammal, "Look, Meenakshi! Muruganar will soon be returning from Palaakkothu. As soon as he enters the hall, you must start singing these verses. But remember one thing! Each of these verses ends with the phrase, 'Ramana Mayavane'. You must substitute 'Muruga Mayavane' for 'Ramana Mayavane' when you sing. Is that clear? Now, take your place and get ready, for Muruganar will be here soon."

Meenakshi Ammal was a simple soul, and her faith in Bhagavan was total. So she agreed to do exactly as Bhagavan said, even though she had no idea why he should want her to do it. Now, the verses selected by Bhagavan were very well suited to the occasion because they presented the picture of a love-lorn lady chiding her lover for his cruel neglect. In these verses, Muruganar portrays himself as a love-lorn lady and entreats Bhagavan to favour him with his grace. To be precise, the lady describes the happy times she had shared with her Lord, and the promises that he had made to her. Having won her with sweet words of love and assurances of undying devotion, her Lord had left her to dream about him, and to wait eagerly for the time when he would come to claim her; but he had not come back. The lady chides her lover for his shameful neglect, and asks him what she had done, to deserve such cruel treatment from him. She bemoans her fate, regretting the fact that she had lost her heart to one so inconsistent, beguiled by his charm and his false promises. Each of the verses ends with the phrase, 'Ramana Mayavane' (the term mayavan can be translated as 'the great deluder'). The lady is accusing her lover of misleading her with false promises. Yet, her language is far from abusive. In fact, her words are full of affection and reflect the remembered joy of happier times. Each of the poems in this section is exquisite in the beauty of expression and the delicacy of feeling.

As soon as Muruganar entered the hall, Meenakshi Ammal started singing the songs selected by Bhagavan. Following Bhagavan's instructions faithfully, she ended each verse with

'Muruga Mayavane' instead of the original 'Ramana Mayavane'. The first time, Muruganar did not attach much importance to the substitution. Many devotees regard Bhagavan as an incarnation of Lord Muruga, and Muruganar simply assumed that Meenakshi Ammal was making a reference to this aspect of Bhagavan's multi-faceted glory. When Meenakshi Ammal came to the end of the second verse and there was still no response from Muruganar, Bhagavan glanced at him with eyes full of mischief. Then he directed a look of approval and encouragement at Meenakshi Ammal. Suddenly, Muruganar realised that some conspiracy was at work! By then, Meenakshi Ammal had ended the third verse also with 'Muruga Mayavane'. This repeated substitution of 'Muruga Mayavane' for 'Ramana Mayavane' now appeared highly significant to Muruganar. He was finally convinced that Bhagavan was deliberately teasing him, using Meenakshi Ammal as an innocent, yet effective agent!

Muruganar could think of only one course of action — Escape! Accordingly, he got up and was preparing to quietly slip out of the hall when Bhagavan stopped him with, "Hey! Why are you leaving the hall now? Is it not because she sang about her 'Muruga Mayavan'? Well, does that mean that, whenever somebody sings about 'Ramana Mayavan', I should immediately walk out of the hall? Is that not so?" Hearing Bhagavan's words, the entire hall dissolved in laughter. Muruganar made use of this diversion to make good his escape!

Bhagavan often played such practical jokes upon his devotees. But even while he was engaged in such apparently playful activities, Bhagavan continued to impart valuable knowledge to his devotees. Every joke and every little trick had its own lesson to teach.

* * *

On one occasion, Muruganar was distributing prasad to the devotees in the hall. Meenakshi Ammal was also in the hall at the time, but she did not receive any of the prasad. After giving the prasad to everyone in the hall, Muruganar went off to the office, to distribute it among the devotees who were there. As soon as Muruganar left the hall, Meenakshi Ammal went to Bhagavan and complained, 'Bhagavan! My husband gave prasad to everyone else, but he did not give any to me.' When Muruganar returned to the hall, Bhagavan took him to task, saying, "What is the matter? Why did you not give any prasad to Meenakshi?" Muruganar answered, "While I was distributing the prasad, everyone held out their hands and I just placed a little of the prasad in each outstretched hand. Meenakshi did not hold out her hand. So it is her own fault that she did not receive the prasad."

Bhagavan now turned to Meenakshi Ammal and asked her, "Meenakshi, did you not hold out your hand like everybody else? Why did you not do so?" Meenakshi Ammal had no reply. The fact was that she had deliberately refrained from holding out her hand, hoping that her husband would notice, and ask her to hold out her hand for the prasad. But Muruganar was not prepared to show her any special favour, and had calmly walked past her. Offended by her husband's coolness, Meenakshi Ammal had then complained to Bhagavan, hoping that Bhagavan would reprimand Muruganar for his negligence. But Muruganar neatly turned the tables on her, thereby leaving her speechless!

Muruganar's love for Bhagavan was so great that, whenever he sat before Bhagavan in the hall, he would keep gazing at him with wide-eyed wonder. His mouth, too, would remain agape, as though he were trying to absorb Bhagavan's enchanting form through every one of his senses.

45. Farewell to Rituals

In the early days of his life at Ramanasramam, Muruganar used to perform the ritualistic ceremonies prescribed for the death anniversaries of his parents. Once, on the day of his mother's anniversary, Muruganar came to the kitchen very early in the morning. He washed his dhoti and hung it up to dry. Then, with a wet towel around his waist, he set about getting the vegetables ready. While Muruganar was thus engaged, Bhagavan entered the kitchen. One glance at the dhoti drying on the clothesline, and the sight of Muruganar clad in a wet towel told Bhagavan everything. He said to Muruganar, "It is your mother's annual ceremony today, is it not? Have you made all arrangements? Who are the Brahmins?" Before Muruganar could reply, Bhagavan himself continued. Tapping himself on the chest, Bhagavan said, "I can be one of the Brahmins. We need one more. I think we can have Ranga Rao as the second Brahmin. Will that be alright?" Muruganar knew well that Bhagavan did not consider rituals important. Yet here he was, making arrangements for the ceremony Muruganar had to perform that day, planning even the smallest details! Muruganar felt so moved that he could hardly keep himself from breaking down completely. Muruganar felt that, at the very instant that Bhagavan tapped his own chest and said, "I will be one of the Brahmins for the ceremony," not only his parents but several generations of his ancestors would have attained Liberation. Muruganar never again felt it necessary to perform the annual ceremony for his parents.

Though Muruganar stopped performing the ceremony, on the next death anniversary of his mother, he brought a large jackfruit, with the intention of giving some fruit to everyone in the Ashram, in memory of his mother. Bhagavan saw Muruganar with the jackfruit and remarked, "It is your mother's anniversary, is it not? I see you have not yet managed to get rid of these sentimental attachments!" Hearing this, Muruganar exclaimed, "I will never do such a thing again." Even belief in rituals can bind one, and Bhagavan was very particular about breaking every one of the ties binding his disciples. Is this not a sure sign of Bhagavan's extraordinary concern for his disciples!

* * *

Once, Bhagavan was talking to Muruganar about certain books. Muruganar was giving Bhagavan a detailed account of the content of each of these books. After listening attentively to all these particulars, Bhagavan remarked, "Ultimately, all these books are saying the same thing. Only the descriptions and illustrations differ from one book to the other. The routes might differ, but the destination is the same." Muruganar readily agreed, saying, "Yes. That is true, after reading all these books, we feel that it has been a waste of time."

Bhagavan replied, "But unless you read the books, how can you get to know that they are all saying the same thing? Until you read them, there would always be the tantalising thought that there might be some new revelation in one book or the other. Only when you have read them can you feel certain that there is nothing to be gained from studying them. This is like saying that one has to perform rituals, before one can truly appreciate the fact that rituals are not needed, or that only through engaging oneself in various forms of worship, one can get to know that performing puja is not very important for spiritual realisation."

46. BHAGAVAN'S GRACE

At first glance, the relationship between Muruganar and Bhagavan might not appear intimate. Luckily for us, Muruganar has recorded many of his experiences in the form of beautiful poems. One such poem recounts the following incident: In the early days, very few devotees stayed with Bhagavan. However, Bhagavan was seldom totally alone. Muruganar had a strong desire to have Bhagavan wholly to himself, at least for a short while. Muruganar never mentioned this yearning to anybody. But can anybody hide anything from Bhagavan? Muruganar's secret wish was fulfilled in a totally unexpected way. In those days, Bhagavan and his devotees used to collect leaves from the trees in the forest, to make leaf-plates. Once, while a party was getting ready to go into the forest, Bhagavan gave Muruganar a very significant glance. Interpreting this look as a signal to follow him, Muruganar hurried after Bhagavan. By the time the others entered the forest, Bhagavan and Muruganar had disappeared into the woods.

Bhagavan led Muruganar deep into the forest. At one place, Bhagavan sat down on a log, and asked Muruganar to sit beside him. Muruganar sat, but no words were exchanged. Bhagavan looked directly into his eyes and Muruganar felt the power of Bhagavan's Grace flowing through him like an electric current. He lost all perceptions of time and space, and experienced a joy beyond description. Immersed in this state of bliss, Muruganar was oblivious to the passage of time; it was only when he regained his senses that he realised that he must have remained in this state of bliss for hours together. Muruganar has mentioned this incident in one of the poems in the section titled *Keerthi Tiru-agaval* in *Sri Ramana Sannidhi Murai*. This verse expresses

Muruganar's gratitude to Bhagavan, for giving him this experience of blissful union with the Self.

Bhagavan himself has corroborated Muruganar's account of this incident. Once, Viswanatha Swami was trying to write a poem. However hard he tried, he was unable to think of anything beyond the phrase: 'Mugavapuri Murugan' and he abandoned the attempt. Bhagavan picked up the same phrase and wrote a verse. Viswanatha Swami saw that Bhagavan had composed a beautiful poem which read as follows: "That Arunachala Ramana, who dwells in the Heart-Lotus, smiled at me and fixed his intent gaze upon me. Through this look of Grace, he totally destroyed my ego and filled my soul with joy. Saying this, Mugavapuri Murugan set about the task of composing *Sri Ramana Sannidhi Murai* which matches the *Tiruvachakam* in its power to confer salvation on all mankind.

Muruganar recounts another anecdote in the same *Keerthi Tiru-agaval* of *Sri Ramana Sannidhi Murai*. He used to stay in Palakothu and go into Tiruvannamalai Town every morning to beg for alms. Sometimes, he would feel disinclined to undertake this trip into town and, on those days, he simply went without food. On several occasions, Muruganar fasted for an entire day. One of these days happened to be the Sivarathri day, though Muruganar himself was not aware of the fact. The next morning, Bhagavan asked Muruganar to go around the Hill with him. Muruganar set off enthusiastically enough but soon, he started feeling the effects of the previous day's starvation. When Bhagavan saw Muruganar's exhaustion, he exclaimed, "Oh! Did you fast yesterday for Sivarathri? See how tired you are now. All right! Now come to the Ashram with me and have a proper meal." Bhagavan took Muruganar to the Ashram and saw to it that he got enough to eat, instructing the attendants to serve

Muruganar with particular care. Muruganar was so moved by Bhagavan's solicitude that even after many years he could not talk about this incident without tears in his eyes.

47. LIBERATION TO PUJA

The Matrubhuteswara Temple, though not particularly large in size, is remarkable for the beauty of its sculptures. It also serves as a model of perfection in that it has been constructed with strict adherence to the time-honoured rules governing temple architecture. The Sri Chakra installed in the sanctum is an extraordinarily powerful one, and its sanctity is enhanced by the daily rituals which are performed with great devotion and attention to detail.

The mortal remains of Bhagavan's mother have been enshrined in this temple, and the Matrubhuteswara Lingam has been installed on the spot. At first, the temple was a very small one, consisting of just one shrine. Later, other idols were installed, and the temple was suitably enlarged. In the early days, the daily ritualistic worship used to be conducted by the devotees in Ramanasramam. In those days, there were very few permanent residents in the Ashram. Whenever he was unable to find anybody else, Chinna Swami would attend to the puja himself.

Once in a while, Chinnaswami would ask Muruganar to conduct the puja. Muruganar could not refuse. Muruganar was a perfectionist and, whatever he did, he would do with whole-hearted concentration. While engaged in one activity, however, he became oblivious of everything else. He also lost track of time, and would often perform a single activity over and over again, any number of times. For example, if he decided to perform the Abhisekham (ritualistic washing) of the idols, he would bring pot after pot of water and pour it over the idols. Then he would start scrubbing the idols, to remove all the accumulated oil and grease. Once, while Muruganar was busy washing the Linga, Bhagavan entered the temple. After watching silently for some time, Bhagavan remarked, in tones of amusement, "The way you scrub that Linga, it looks as though the entire stone image might disappear within a few days' time!"

On another occasion, Bhagavan happened to enter the temple just as Muruganar was finishing the day's puja. At the end of the puja, the customary practice is to perform the *Aarati* (worship of the deity with lighted lamps and burning camphor). Muruganar placed a lump of camphor on a plate, and lighted it and picked up the bell in his left hand and started ringing it. While ringing the bell he could not perform *Aarati*. He was experiencing difficulty in doing both simultaneously. In consternation, he started mumbling to himself, "I wonder how others manage to recite the mantras, ring the bell with one hand, and keep up the circular motion of the *Aarati* plate with the other hand, all at the same time! It requires such perfect synchronisation of activities! I suppose it is a gift that other people possess. I myself can never master this art!"

At this, Bhagavan teased him, "Oh! Your performance is simply amazing! I have been admiring you all this while. How nicely you ring the bell! And the graceful manner in which you perform the Aarati is simply beyond description!"

Muruganar was startled to hear Bhagavan's voice, for he had not noticed him entering the temple. When he realised that Bhagavan must have been watching him for a long time, he was thoroughly embarrassed. He said, "Bhagavan! I am not going to perform puja any more. This is quite beyond my capabilities! I am going to tell Chinnaswami that I just cannot do this." Bhagavan smiled broadly and said, "That is good. Now you have granted liberation to *puja*!"

48. AN IDEAL HOME LIFE

In the early days, there were very few permanent residents in the Ashram, and the Ashram itself was just a simple, small affair. In those days, Bhagavan used to work in the kitchen every morning, guiding and assisting the kitchen workers. Bhagavan's intimate devotees treasured these quiet early morning hours in the kitchen, because of the opportunity to work in close proximity to Bhagavan.

One morning, Bhagavan was chopping greens. Muruganar was sitting close to Bhagavan and was engaged in the same task. Bhagavan was recounting anecdotes of his days on the Hill. He was talking about the various kinds of herbs found on the Hill and about the properties of each kind. He told stories about how he had climbed the tamarind tree and plucked the tender leaves so that the 'Greens-granny' could cook them for him. He talked about the old lady's amazing knowledge about the properties of every kind of herb that grew upon the Hill. Bhagavan recalled that the old lady would say, "This leaf is good for your eye-sight. This one has cooling properties and so, if you eat it regularly, you need not apply oil on your head to cool your system. This one is very effective as a laxative" and so on.

Bhagavan continued: "There are several rare herbs to be found on the Arunachala Hill. It is said that some of these herbs can wipe out sensation of hunger and thirst and that sages used to take these herbs so that they could perform penance for years together without being bothered by hunger and thirst. Some of the herbs are supposed to bestow longevity, and it is believed that these helped sages to live for several centuries! There is even a belief that, with the help of some herbs, one could acquire the power to transport oneself through space, and reach any place of one's choice just by thinking about it!"

Muruganar was fascinated by Bhagavan's words and completely forgot the work on hand. Bhagavan finished his portion of the job and with the intention of stacking all the greens together, and gathering all the roots into one single heap, he looked at Muruganar's workspot and remarked, "Look at him! He is really very smart! Muruganar, your skill in chopping greens is as striking as your success in running a household!" (Muruganar's extraordinary 'domestic skills' are, of course, well known to all of us!)

Bhagavan's remark jolted Muruganar out of his trance-like state. He looked down at his handiwork. The few stalks he had managed to chop were lying scattered all over the place. The roots were in an even messier state, lying like wounded soldiers on a battlefield! Then he looked at Bhagavan's portion of the work and saw the chopped greens piled up neatly in one place, with the roots in a separate heap. Even the roots had been laid in a neat pile! Not a scrap had been wasted; nothing was out of place. Muruganar was quite ashamed of himself. As if to add insult to injury, Bhagavan was now making fun of his clumsy attempts at helping in the kitchen! What could poor Muruganar do? He could think of only one form of retaliation. He went out, took a piece of paper, wrote something on it and, left the paper on Bhagavan's sofa. As soon as Bhagavan entered the hall, he picked up the piece of paper and read it. Seeing the smile of amusement as he read, the devotees in the hall asked him what was on the piece of paper. Bhagavan handed the paper to the nearest person and said, "Here, read it yourself."

This devotee had not been in the kitchen that morning and so, he had no idea of the incident referred to in the poem. He requested Bhagavan to explain. Bhagavan said, 'Muruganar was helping me chop vegetables this morning and I teased him about his lack of skill in domestic chores. I told him that he chopped the greens with the same efficiency with which he managed his household. In reply to my remarks, he has written this poem. The gist of the poem is, "O Ramana! You are an extraordinarily efficient person. Why don't you marry an equally efficient young lady and set up house? Why should you be wandering around as a mendicant in loin cloth, begging food when you could so easily have set up an ideal household?" (v.863)

49. THE LIZARD DEVOTION

Muruganar regarded Bhagavan with as much reverent awe as loving devotion. To Muruganar, Bhagavan's smallest wish was a command to be carried out without the slightest delay. When in Bhagavan's presence, Muruganar would be sitting with his eyes wide open. He would be so absorbed in his contemplation of Bhagavan's captivating form that he would be unaware of anything else. In fact, whenever Bhagavan happened to look for Muruganar, in order to get some writing done, the other devotees would wake Muruganar from his trance and draw his attention to the fact that Bhagavan wanted his assistance.

Once, Muruganar had just prostrated to Bhagavan when Bhagavan asked him some question regarding some literary work. Still lying on the floor, Muruganar just lifted up his head alone, and answered Bhagavan's query. Only after giving Bhagavan a detailed account of the matter did he get up from the floor.

Viswanatha Swami, who was in the hall at the time, was quite amazed by Murugnar's behaviour. When Muruganar left the hall, Viswanatha Swami followed him outside and, said to Muruganar, "What is this! Your behaviour is strange indeed! When Bhagavan speaks to you, do you not have to stand up and listen to him with respectful attention? How can you lie on the floor with your head raised, like a lizard, while Bhagavan is talking to you?"

Muruganar was very much upset when he heard this. In a faltering voice, he said, "You are right. I should not have spoken to Bhagavan while lying on the floor. But when Bhagavan speaks to me, I forget everything else except the fact that Bhagavan is asking me a question and that I should answer it immediately. In the urgency of the moment, I cannot think about whether I am standing, sitting or lying down. What can I do?" Seeing how deeply upset Muruganar was, Viswanatha Swami realised the depth of his feelings, and could not say anything further. However, he couldn't resist the temptation to tease Muruganar for what he termed his 'lizard devotion'!

50. Seize the Opportunity

In the early days, items of daily use, like tooth-powder and medicinal oils were prepared in the Ashram itself. The herbs and other ingredients were available locally and the devotees were able to obtain everything easily. Bhagavan used to play an active part in the preparation of herbal tonics and medicinal oils. He knew the recipes for all the preparations, and has recorded the recipes, specifying the exact quantity of each ingredient to be used in each preparation, together with the method of preparation. Each time some medicinal powder or tonic or herbal oil was prepared in the Ashram kitchen, Bhagavan would personally supervise the operation, provide information and guidance also.

Once, a particular oil was being prepared. The herbs were measured and mixed according to Bhagavan's instructions, and the mixture was placed on the stove to boil. When the process of preparation was nearing completion, Bhagavan was informed, and asked to come and check on it. On his way to the cowshed, Bhagavan came to the kitchen. He found that the oil was ready to be removed from the fire and so he asked the attendants to place the container on the floor and allow the hot oil to cool. After a while, Bhagavan came back to the kitchen to see to the filtration and storage of the oil.

A large vessel was placed on the floor and a white cloth was spread across the mouth of the vessel. Bhagavan held the cloth in place, and Muruganar started transferring oil from the cauldron to the vessel, using a mug. As the work was going on, Bhagavan was telling Muruganar about the various herbs that had been used in the preparation, about the specific qualities of each herb, and the benefits to be derived from the prepared oil.

Muruganar was apt to forget everything at the mere sight of Bhagavan. Now, with Bhagavan in such close proximity and talking about such interesting things, Muruganar was totally lost. He forgot all about his surroundings and the work he was supposed to be doing. His mind was totally engrossed in Bhagavan's words, but his hands mechanically continued the task of pouring oil from one vessel into the other. The vessel was full, but Muruganar did not notice that. Bhagavan, however, was alert as ever and said, "Look out! The vessel is full. Didn't you notice?" At Bhagavan's words, Muruganar was jolted back to his senses, but not quickly enough. In his confusion, he poured one more mug of oil into the vessel and it promptly overflowed.

Muruganar was dismayed to see the oil streaming along the floor. Bhagavan laughed at the bewildered expression on his face and said to him, "Don't let the oil go to waste. Who is going to supply you with such a nice herbal oil? Quick, take it and rub it on your scalp, it will do you good!"

Immediately, Muruganar started scooping up the oil from the floor and rubbing it on his head. He was still in a dazed state, and was not fully aware of what he was doing. He knew only that Bhagavan had asked him to take the oil from the floor and apply it on his head. He proceeded to do just that, with his hand travelling mechanically from floor to head and back to the floor. Even after all the oil was gone, he continued repeating the same sequence of actions, with the result that he was now scooping up the mud and rubbing it on his head! Only when Bhagavan burst out laughing, "Hey! I told you to apply only the oil, not the mud!", did Muruganar realise what he was doing. With a shamefaced look, he finally stopped! All the while Sri Bhagavan was holding the cloth and it did not occur to Muruganar that he should help Bhagavan remove the cloth from the vessel. Finally Subbalakshmi Ammal who was doing some work in the kitchen had to relieve Bhagavan and finish the job on hand.

* * *

While Muruganar was teaching me the works of Bhagavan, he used to quote extensively from the scriptures and other ancient texts. In the course of one of these sessions, Muruganar said to me, "The ancient texts tell us about the incidents that took place in previous ages. Everything that happens during our own lifetime, we regard as current news. Those incidents that took place in the past, but within a certain time-frame, we classify as history. When we hear accounts of what took place in even earlier times, we are unable to believe the authenticity of those accounts. Yet, at the time those events occurred, they too must have been 'current events'!

Veda Vyasa, the author of the Mahabharatha, has talked about our present age (Kali Yuga). In the Srimad Bhagavatha, Vyasa has clearly stated that, during the Kali Yuga, human beings can attain Liberation through very easy means, like chanting of the Divine Names and the proximity of Realised Souls. In the *Arunachala Mahatmyam*, we find the declaration that the mere sight of the Arunachala Hill is enough to grant Liberation. Further it states that, if one is unable to go to Arunachala, one just has to think of Arunachala with sincere devotion and the thought alone is sufficient to bestow Liberation! In ancient times like the Krita Yuga, Threta Yuga and Dwapara Yuga, Liberation could be attained only through rigorous penance and unswerving devotion to one's Guru. But we, in this Kali Yuga, are assured of Liberation through much easier practices. Are we not in an enviably fortunate position!

We now have difficulty in believing that the incidents recorded in the ancient books are authentic. In the same way, in coming ages, people are likely to find it difficult to believe the accounts of Sri Bhagavan's life and teachings. That the young Venkataraman realised the Great Truth, merely by concentrating on the question of 'what is it that dies?', and that he was able to attain Self Realisation without any formal training or the instructions of a Guru — these facts are certainly too wonderful to be readily believed! It is certain that in future ages, saints and sages will tell the story of Sri Ramana Maharshi to their disciples, and those disciples will listen with the same awe and wonder with which we listen to the *Ramayana* and the *Mahabharata* now!" Even as he spoke these words, Muruganar's eyes filled with tears and his voice became hoarse with emotion.

We can certainly say that, just as Bhagavan's life and teachings are sure to provide future generations with inspiration, Muruganar's devotion to Bhagavan will also serve as an enduring model for ages to come.

51. MASSAGE THAT PILLAR

Venkataratnam was one of Bhagavan's personal attendants. He was a young graduate with quiet, unassuming manners. He was very devoted to Bhagavan. He was a bachelor and had dedicated himself to Bhagavan's service.

In those days, visitors took up Bhagavan's time and attention throughout the daytime. All day long, Bhagavan would be engaged in giving darshan to devotees, in clarifying their doubts, and in giving advice on spiritual matters.

But the nights belonged to Bhagavan's personal attendants! The night times can be considered the precious reward for the attendants' day-long labours. It was during the quiet hours of the late evening that Bhagavan lavished all his attention on his attendants. He would tell them interesting stories of the great saints and seers of olden days. He would narrate tales from Periapuranam, Bhaktha Vijayam etc. Bhagavan had the ability to hold his listeners spell bound. Not only were his descriptions strikingly vivid, Bhagavan would also imitate the words and gestures of characters, with the perfection of a gifted actor and mimic. So much so that the listeners found themselves being transported back in time and space, actually 'living' the story that Bhagavan was recounting!

Once, Bhagavan was in the Hall with a small group of devotees around him. The evening meal was over, and the Ashram was quiet. Venkataratnam sat at Bhagavan's feet, and started massaging Bhagavan's legs, to relieve the arthritic pain. One of the devotees said to Bhagavan, "We know that Saint Namadeva was very devoted to Lord Pandarinatha. Yet, Pandarinatha sent him to Jnanadeva for religious instruction. Why is it that the Lord did not directly involve Himself with Namadeva's spiritual progress?"

In response to this query, Bhagavan told us the following story: "One day, Gorakumbha invited Jnanadeva, Namadeva and a few other holy men to his house. In the course of his conversation with Gorakumbha, Jnanadeva said, 'Sir, you are an expert at pottery work. You can easily differentiate between a half-baked pot and a perfectly baked one. Why don't you examine all of us?' Gorakumbha got up and walked along the lines of holy men, tapping each on the head with his knuckles. . . " At this point, Bhagavan acted out the part of Gorakumbha, miming the gestures of a person tapping and listening, then tapping again on the next head. All the devotees were enthralled. Venkatratnam was as engrossed in the story as the rest of the people. In fact, he was so caught up in the story that he had forgotten he was at Ramanasramam, and had been transported into Gorakumbha's house! He was no longer aware of the task he was supposed to be engaged in. Suddenly, feeling Bhagavan's eyes upon him, Venkataratnam recalled his surroundings and recollected the fact that he was massaging Bhagavan's legs. When he noticed Bhagavan looking at him, Venkataratnam thought,

"Bhagavan must have been checking to see whether I am paying attention to the story."

Bhagavan continued with his narration. Venkataratnam once again lost himself in the story. Once more, Bhagavan gave Venkataratnam an intent look. The young man was now convinced that he had been shamefully negligent, and started pressing Bhagavan's leg with all his strength. Bhagavan went on with his narration, but was forced to stop after a little while. He suddenly drew up his legs and said to Venkataratnam, "Look! All that you want is something to press with your hands, is it not? Go and press that pillar! Massage it to your heart's content!"

Only then did Venkataratnam realise what he had been doing. In his preoccupation with the story, he had been massaging the same spot, pressing into the tender flesh of Bhagavan's calves. As the story became more and more interesting, he had become correspondingly more and more excited, and had pressed even harder! The pain must have been severe, and that is why Bhagavan had paused in his narration two or three times and looked at Venkataratnam. But he was so absorbed in the story that he was totally unaware of his own actions. In fact, he had been so distracted that he had completely misinterpreted Bhagavan's glances. When he realised the extent of his mistake, Venkataratnam was beside himself with remorse. He was thoroughly ashamed of himself. He spent a sleepless night. The next day, Venkataratnam hesitated to go anywhere near Bhagavan. He was afraid that Bhagavan might be displeased with his thoughtless behaviour.

Being the very embodiment of compassion, Bhagavan could not remain unresponsive to his devotee's heartfelt remorse and regret. Bhagavan himself called Venkataratnam to his side and said to him, in a gentle voice, "Why are you feeling so bad? There is no need to feel ashamed of yourself. Anyone in your position would have done exactly what you did. Forget it and don't worry." Bhagavan's gentle tone and his understanding words set Venkataratnam's troubled heart at rest.

52. Rishaba Vahanam

During Deepam Festival days, the deity is decorated beautifully and brought out in procession through the four streets around the temple. Each day, Lord Arunachala rides on different Mounts. Of these, the great silver Rishaba (Sacred Bull) that bears the Lord on the fifth day of the festival is very special. This silver *Rishaba* is gigantic in size and unmatched in beauty. The Bull appears to be fully conscious of the great privilege that has been bestowed upon it, and moves through the streets with a proud look on its radiant face. The temple priests seem to have a special love for this particular ceremonial mount. They decorate it with evident pride in their own artistic creativity. The flower garlands and the huge flower umbrella are made with great attention to detail. Even the bulls that draw the majestic *Rishaba* (now all the Mounts are pulled with tractor) through the streets are bedecked with colourful garlands of beads and flowers.

Once, Venkatratnam went to the temple to see the *Rishaba Vahana*. The procession started a little later than usual, because it took a rather long time to install the deity on the back of the huge *Rishaba*. The procession itself was an engrossing affair, with *Nagaswara* experts playing sweet music, and with spectacular firework displays at every street corner. By the time the procession had covered the entire route and returned to the temple, it was quite late. So Venkataratnam did not go back to the Ashram, but spent the rest of the night in a friend's house. Next morning, he went to the Ashram and resumed his regular duties. As soon as Bhagavan saw him, he asked, "You were not here last night. Did you go to the temple?" Venkataratnam said, "Yes, Bhagavan." He would have stopped with that, had not Bhagavan exclaimed, "Is not the *Rishaba Vahanam* a grand sight!" This encouraged Venkataratnam to give a more detailed account of his experiences.

He enthusiastically described the *Rishaba* and the elaborate decorations. "Bhagavan! The *Rishaba* is so huge, and its appearance is so majestic! Oh, what lovely garlands it wore on its neck! And what a grand flower-umbrella it bore! Even the bulls that drew the carriage were beautifully decorated. What colourful garlands they had on their necks! They even had multi-coloured balloons tied to their horns!"

Bhagavan said, "Yes! Yes! Everything would have been very grand yesterday. There must have been an extraordinarily large garland of flowers also. Did you notice that?" Venkataratnam replied, "Yes, Bhagavan! It was enormous! They say that it is made especially for the Lord to wear on the fifth day of the festival. Do you know Bhagavan, the priests had to climb up a ladder just to place the garland around the deity? In addition to all this, there were coloured bulbs strung around the head and the sides of the *Rishaba*. With the twinkling lights and the colourful garlands, not to mention the glittering ornaments, the *Rishaba* Vahana was indeed a grand sight!"

Bhagavan interrupted the excited flow of words with a question: "Where were you standing? Could you see everything clearly from where you stood?"

Venkataratnam said, "It was terribly crowded Bhagavan. It would have been impossible to see everything from the same spot. At first, I watched from within the Mandapam. Then I moved to the corner beside the peanut stall. When the *Rishaba* came out of the temple and turned the corner, I had a clear view. What a splendid sight it was! And the fire-works were superb. What dazzling brilliance and what ear-splitting explosions! It is impossible to describe it all in words. No wonder that it is famous all over India! No wonder such a huge crowd had gathered to witness it! The crowd was like a surging sea. It was so difficult to get out of it in one piece!"

Having listened to all this, Bhagavan asked, "You have said so much about the crowd and the decorations and everything else. But you have not said a single word about Arunachala Himself. Well, how was He?"

Venkataratnam replied, "All the elaborate preparations and the spectacular arrangements were for Him, were they not? Everything is for Him alone!" Bhagavan said, "You said that the garland was huge, you said so much about the intricate patterns on the flower umbrella, you said the carriage was drawn by bulls and you even described the garlands around the bulls' necks. But you have not talked about Arunachala at all! That is why I asked. Maybe you feel that it is not necessary to talk about Him. After all, He is always the same, is He not? Perhaps that is why you did not mention Him at all!"

Only then did poor Venkataratnam realise that Bhagavan had been teasing him deliberately. Bhagavan had encouraged, questioned and provoked him into giving such an impassioned account of the previous night's experiences. Venkataratnam had obligingly talked at length about all the other details, but had forgotten all about Arunachala! Bhagavan's query jolted Venkataratnam out of his absorption in the inessential details and made him realise that he had allowed the inessential details to take up all his attention, thus distracting him from the essential. Even though Bhagavan appeared to be just having some fun at

Vekataratnam's expense, there was actually a very important lesson underlying it all. It is a lesson all of us should learn, because every one of us, at some time or the other, makes the same mistake as Venkataratnam. We often allow the inessential and the ephemeral to take up all our attention, thereby losing sight of the One Everlasting Truth. Bhagavan often taught the most profound truths through apparently light-hearted remarks.

53. WHY LEAVE MADURAI AT ALL?

Once, a young man came to the Ashram. He was about twenty years old. He entered the Jubilee Hall and made his way through the crowd of devotees, to stand before Bhagavan with folded hands. Bhagavan looked at the youth with a gracious smile. The young man asked, "Bhagavan, while one is engaged in Nama *Japa* (chanting of God's Name), is it better to say 'Rama' or 'Krishna' or could one combine both, and say 'Rama-krishna'?" Bhagavan replied, "Every Name is equally potent. You can chant any Name singly or in combination. Whether you say 'Rama', 'Krishna' or 'Ramakrishna', the effect is the same. What is important is the degree of mental concentration you are able to achieve and sustain."

Next, the youth asked, "Is it alright to do such japam in one's house itself, or is it necessary to leave home and go to an Ashram or some secluded spot?" Bhagavan said, "There is no need to leave your home and look for a suitable spot. Spiritual practices can be carried out wherever convenient. Your house is as good a place as any other."

Then he asked, "If that is so, then why did Bhagavan leave Madurai and come to Tiruvannamalai? Was not Madurai a good enough place?" Bhagavan sat up straight and said, "So! This is what you have in your mind, is it? You are wondering why I should have left home, if one place is really as good as any other place. But you should note one thing. I did not go around asking people, 'Should I stay here or should I go somewhere else?' I just did what I felt like doing. If you also have a strong feeling that you should leave home, why don't you do so? If your conviction is strong enough, you will not feel the need for other people's approval or support." The young man appeared to be at a loss for words. The young man stood silently for a few moments and then left the hall.

After the youth left the place, Bhagavan said to the devotees around, "This boy has no confidence or the courage to face the consequences. He is afraid that, if he were to leave the security of his home, he might not be able to fend for himself. It is only the weak-minded people who go around asking for other people's advice. The strong-willed ones just do what their heart says is right. Such strength of character is a God-given gift. Total self-reliance is not possible without His Grace."

54. VARANASI SUBBULAKSHMI AMMAL

Varanasi Subbulakshmi Ammal was a devotee of Bhagavan. She hailed from the Nellore District of Andhra Pradesh. She was widowed at a very young age and lost all interest in worldly matters. She decided to dedicate herself to spiritual pursuits and spent all her time engaged in reading philosophical books, and in *Nama Japa* and meditation.

As a young girl, Subbulakshmi Ammal had come to Tiruvannamalai with her mother when Bhagavan was staying in Virupaksha Cave. When she was about 31 years old, she again came on her way back from Rameswaram, where she had gone with a group of people. When she reached Tiruvannamalai, she remembered her earlier visit, and was eager to see Bhagavan again. She made enquiries, and learned that Bhagavan had settled in the present Ashram. The group came to Ramanasramam and sat in the meditation hall for some time. Then, they all took leave of Bhagavan and proceeded on their pilgrimage.

On her third visit, she stayed in Bhagavan's presence for half a day and did *giripradakshinam* before leaving for Kalahasti. That night she dreamt that a priest of her acquaintance came to her and told her, 'Tiruvannamalai is the right place for you. Bhagavan Sri Ramana, the Omniscient One, will show you the way to Liberation. Go to him and surrender.' She felt that the dream was a message from God. So she came back to Tiruvannamalai and took a house for rent. Now it was possible for her to visit Ramanasramam regularly. She often discussed her spiritual aspirations with Bhagavan and he graciously cleared her doubts and guided her. The Ashram authorities invited her to come and stay in the Ashram, but she was unwilling due to her orthodoxy. Once, it so happened that Shanthammal was left to manage all the work in the Ashram kitchen. At that time, Chinnaswami requested Subbulakshmi Ammal to help out. Subbulakshmi Ammal readily agreed, and was amply rewarded for her generosity, because Bhagavan spent a lot of time, guiding and advising those in the kitchen. Subbulakshmi Ammal was an avid reader. Once, while reading *Bhaktha Vijayam*, she came across a passage that stated Lord Panduranga used to dine with the Saint Namadeva, and that Namadeva conversed with the Lord as with a friend. Subbulakshmi Ammal was very much impressed and waited for an opportunity to ask Bhagavan about this.

One morning, just after breakfast, Bhagavan was sitting in the dining hall. There was no one else nearby. Subbulakshmi

Ammal seized the opportunity. She went up to Bhagavan with a glass of hot water. Giving him the glass, she stood before Bhagavan and asked, "Bhagavan, it is said that Namadeva used to talk freely with Lord Panduranga and that the Lord would sit next to Namadeva and eat with him, just like a friend. Is it really possible for anybody to be on such intimate terms with God? Is it true that God was actually there, in human form?" Bhagavan looked at her and said, "Yes. That is what is written in the book, and whatever the book says is as true as the fact that you and I are now here, and conversing with each other. If this is real, then the statements made in the book are real too. If this is unreal, then the claims made in the book are also unreal. Everything depends upon the imagination! Once the devotee becomes absorbed in the Self, he stops thinking of God as being separate from himself. But until he reaches such a state, one must keep his faith alive. God has to grant the devotee's every prayer, to coax him to stay on the path of Self-realisation. Once Realisation is attained, the devotee loses his sense of individuality and merges with the Supreme Being. Now he knows that everything is but a manifestation of the Self." All her doubts disappeared when she heard Bhagavan's clear and precise explanation. She felt that her mind had gained a greater clarity.

55. Singular Taste

The Bose Compound (Mahasthan) is situated opposite to the Palakothu, close to Ramanasramam. This was built by Aravind Bose, one of Bhagavan's devotees. Bose's mother was very old. In spite of her age and infirmity, the lady visited the Ashram everyday, and spent some time with Bhagavan and his devotees.

Echamma and Mudaliar Patti used to bring food for Bhagavan every day. Seeing this, Bose's mother developed the desire to cook something herself and offer it to Bhagavan. For a while, she hesitated to tell Bhagavan about this, but eventually, she found the courage to inform Bhagavan of her intentions. Bhagavan tried to dissuade the old lady saying, "There is no need for all that. There are people to take care of these details. You are older than I am. Why should you strain yourself unnecessarily? It is enough that you come here every day and spend your time with all of us." But the old lady was determined to have her way. So she went to the Ashram Office and somehow managed to obtain permission to bring food for Bhagavan and his devotees the next day.

She prepared a number of dishes and, with the help of a servant boy, she brought all the food to the Ashram kitchen to serve Bhagavan with her own hands.

Bhagavan entered the hall, and sat down in his customary place. The lady served Bhagavan with her own hands. As she served each item, she told Bhagavan all about the preparation, and the special benefits that particular item could bestow upon the body. After she had served each item on Bhagavan's plate, the Ashram attendants took the vessel and served all the other people in the dining hall, as she was too old to do so herself.

Bhagavan gave the signal for everybody to start eating. He then mixed all the items on his plate, and started eating. This was always Bhagavan's practice. He never tasted each item separately, or expressed any preferences or dislike for anything. This particular day, Bhagavan saw that the old lady had brought a large variety of dishes, and had carefully served each item separately on his plate. Looking at a devotee who was nearby, Bhagavan said, "You know

Hindi, do you not? Please tell this lady that there is no need for her to take so much trouble. At her age, it must have been a great strain, making so many different items. Poor thing! She might have expected me to appreciate each item. But I never taste each item separately. I do not require variety. My taste is 'singular'. All I need is the One! Please tell this lady not to put herself to so much trouble in future."

Bhagavan often used the most ordinary situations to illustrate lofty ideas. Once, during lunch, Subbulakshmi was trying to coax him to take a second helping of vegetable stew. She said, "Bhagavan does not eat anything that is hot and spicy. This stew is bland in taste. Please let me serve a little more of it." Bhagavan was not convinced, however! He said, "You have already served some of it on my plate. Is that not enough? Do I have to eat everything with this one mouth alone? Am I not partaking of every item through so many mouths? What more is required?" Though this remark was made in a casual manner, it serves as an illustration of Bhagavan's infiniteness. His total absorption in the Self resulted in his recognition of the many as no more than illusory aspects of the 'One'.

56. Life is Governed by Prarabdha

Once, Bhagavan and his devotees were discussing *Jnanachara Vichara Padalam* in *Devikalottara* (*Collected Works*). The discussion was mainly about the idea expressed in one particular verse, namely, the idea of total detachment of the mind from the physical body.

Bhagavan said, "Our acts of commission and omission in past lives determine the course of this present life. The physical body has to go through certain pre-ordained experiences. Once it has undergone the experiences ordained for that particular lifetime, the body drops off automatically. There is no need for a person to feel frustrated about the difficulties in taking care of the body. At the same time, there is no need to become anybody's slave, just to ensure nourishment for the body. Then, how is the body to be nourished?" He then proceeded to narrate the following story, to illustrate this point:

"Hiranyakasipu was the king of the *asuras* (demons). Hiranyakasipu's son, Prahlada was however, far from being demonic in his nature. Prahlada, from his earliest days was chanting the potent *mantra* "Om Namo Narayanaya". The demon king had subjugated all the gods and demigods. But he was powerless to stop his own son from chanting the Divine Name. The demon king was furious because his son insisted upon singing the praises of his own deadly enemy- Lord Narayana, but could not do anything about it. When it was time for Prahlada to go to school, Hiranyakasipu called Chandamarkan, who ran the Royal School, and ordered him, "My son has somehow developed the habit of chanting the name of my enemy. It is your duty to persuade him to give up that practice, and to make him chant 'Om Namo Hiranyakashyapaya' instead." Chandamarka took the young prince to his school in the forest, with the royal command ringing in his ears.

Early the next morning, all the pupils gathered in the schoolroom. As soon as their teacher arrived, all the students stood up for the morning prayers. Prahalada got up with the others. Chandamarka led his students in chanting, 'Om Namo Hiranyakashyapaya'. But a lone voice intoned, 'Om Namo Narayanaya'. Chandamarka took the young prince by the hand, led him away from the other boys, and spoke to him gently, "My dear child, you must not chant that name in this place.

This is the realm of the demons and as you know, your father is the all-powerful king of the demons. Narayana is your father's sworn enemy. Any mention of his enemy's name will only enrage your father. Please join the other students in this show of loyalty to the King of the land. It will please your father greatly if you learn to chant 'Om Namo Hiranyakashyapaya'."

Prahlada listened to his teacher in total silence. Chandamarka took Prahlada's silence as a sign of approval and agreement. He was quite sure that he had succeeded in convincing the young prince. But Prahlada continued to chant the name of Lord Narayana. Not only did Prahlada refuse to change his ways, he even managed to convert the other students to his own way of thinking. There was something irresistibly attractive about the young prince, and the other boys just could not stay away from him. Whenever their teacher was away from the schoolroom, the other children would gather around Prahlada. He would tell them about the greatness of Narayana and teach them to chant His Name. On his return to the classroom, Chandamarka was astounded by the sight of all the children chanting 'Om Namo Narayanaya' in unison. He knew that he could not do anything with Prahlada, but he believed that the other children would be easier to deal with. So he said to the other boys, "Soon you must go out into the world and earn your livelihood. How can you prosper in life if the king is displeased with you? By disobeying the royal command, you will surely earn the wrath of the king, and that will ruin your prospects in life."

Nevertheless, they could not resist the charm of Prahlada. The next time the teacher was away from the class, the boys again gathered around Prahlada. When he asked them to chant the Name of Narayana, one of the bolder boys protested, saying, "It is all very well for you to disregard the king's commands. You are the prince of this land and so, you need not worry about making a living. But we are not like that. We will lose our livelyhood. Knowing this, why do you ask us to disobey the king?"

Prahlada smiled at the boy and said, "Did you come into the world with the king's permission? Does the king really have power over your life? You did not enter this world at the king's command. You were born so that you could fulfil the decrees of Fate. Even before you were born, the entire course of your life was determined to the smallest detail. King Hiranyakasipu has power only in this land, whereas Lord Narayana rules the entire universe. We have to come into the world again and again, in order to experience the fruits of our past deeds. The only way to break the chains of Fate is to gain the favour of Narayana. He alone has the power to free you from all bondage. Devote your life to earning His Grace, so that you can be free forever!"

57. THE WHITE PEACOCK

Some devotees believe that Bhagavan was the incarnation of Lord Subrahmanya. Many incidents in Bhagavan's life seem to substantiate this belief. Lord Muruga's Mount is the peacock. Sri Ramanasramam is full of peacocks and Bhagavan was often surrounded by these beautiful birds. As his usual, Bhagavan was always especially gracious to the peacocks. He always kept some tasty tid-bits for them, and fed them lovingly whenever they chose to visit him. The Ashram peacocks seemed to know that they were specially privileged birds, and would strut about as though they owned the place! While Bhagavan was in the Jubilee Hall, the peacocks were very happy, because they could approach Bhagavan from any direction, at any time.

It was a common sight in the Ashram, for a peacock to pick its way through the crowd of devotees, to receive a fruit or nut from Bhagavan's hands. The peacocks were on such intimate terms with Bhagavan that it often seemed like they knew his daily routine perfectly, and arranged their own activities accordingly! When Bhagavan went to the cowshed in the morning, a peacock would be waiting for him by the side of the path. When Bhagavan caught sight of the peacock, he would stand still and gaze at the bird. It would also gaze back. After a while, the bird would turn and go away, as though satisfied with the meeting. To us, it seemed as though some sublime communication had taken place, between Bhagavan and the bird.

In 1947, the Maharani of Baroda sent a white peacock to Ramanasramam. Bhagavan observed, "The other peacocks are indeed beautiful, with their brilliant colouring and their spectacular feathers, but this white peacock has a unique beauty of its own. Its white feathers seem to be a symbol of purity."

From the time the white peacock arrived in the Ashram, Bhagavan made it a point to sleep in the Jubilee hall. A cage was erected next to Bhagavan's stone couch, and the white peacock stayed in this enclosure through the night time. All the other peacocks roosted in the trees throughout the night, and came into the hall at the crack of dawn, to see Bhagavan. The white peacock alone had the unique privilege of staying near Bhagavan all through the night.

Soon it was winter, and Bhagavan's personal attendants felt that it would be advisable to shift Bhagavan's bed into the hall. As Bhagavan sometimes had asthmatic attacks, the attendants were concerned about the effect of the cold breezes upon his health. But when they requested Bhagavan to move into the hall, he refused. No amount of persuasion could convince him to change his mind. Bhagavan said, "The white peacock has come to us from a far-away place. He might not be quite comfortable in these surroundings. How can I abandon him and seek comfort for myself alone? When a guest comes to our house, would it be proper to make him sleep outside, while we ourselves occupied the bedroom? The right thing to do would be to offer the guest all comforts. If that is not possible, we should at least refrain from enjoying all the comforts ourselves. The most courteous thing to do would be to share the verandah with your guest." Many of Bhagavan's devotees believed that Madhava Swami, an attendant who had served Bhagavan faithfully for many years was reborn as the white peacock. Bhagavan too addressed the white peacock as Madhava.

G.V.Subbaramaiah, one of Bhagavan's devotees, was so struck by the extraordinary relationship between Bhagavan and the white peacock that he composed a poem, titled *Svetha-mayura-ashtakam*. Bhagavan read the eight stanzas, gave the poem to Lalitha Venkataraman and asked her to play the verses on her veena. Lalitha studied the poem and prepared to set the tune to play on the veena. Just as she was about to start playing, Bhagavan exclaimed, "Wait! The hero of the poem is not here. We should get him here, to listen to the song which has been composed in his honour." So saying, Bhagavan raised his voice and called, "Madhava! Where are you?" Immediately, the peacock flew down from the roof of the hall and stood before his Master. Bhagavan's face shone like the full moon at this.

The lady started singing the verses and playing the veena. As soon as she started singing, the peacock spread its tail and started dancing. It continued to dance, all the while she sang. As soon as she stopped playing, the peacock went up to her and pecked at the strings of the Veena. Bhagavan laughed at the peacock's antics, and said to Lalitha, "Madhavan wants you to repeat the singing." She immediately started singing once again. This time also, the peacock danced through the performance! It was a truly thrilling experience for all of us.

On one occasion, when the white peacock was walking around the hall freely, without showing any signs of timidity among so many people, a devotee remarked, "Surely this bird must have been closely associated with this place in its last birth. Otherwise, would it be possible for any bird to mingle so freely with people, forgetting its natural timidity?" Bhagavan said, "You are right. This bird really is extraordinary in its behaviour. That is why everybody here says that this peacock must be Madhavan." The devotee asked, "Does that mean that the bird actually remembers its past life?" To this, Bhagavan replied, "No, no! That is not possible. It is difficult enough to deal with the troubles and worries of one life at a time. How can anyone survive the strain of all the conflicting thoughts and emotions of a series of lives! It is true that the experiences of each lifetime are determined by the actions performed in previous lives. But nobody remembers the details of his past lives. God, in His mercy, has blessed us with forgetfulness or Tirobhavam (the divine illusion through concealment.)

The white peacock's attachment to Bhagavan was certainly remarkable. During the last hours of Bhagavan's life in the body, the peacock sat on the roof of the Nirvana room and rent the air with its plaintive cries. The bird's mournful cries were an expression of its anguish and sorrow, so full of feeling as to melt the hardest heart. Bhagavan often remarked that great souls could appear in our midst, in unexpected garbs. If someone was unkind to an animal or a bird, Bhagavan would chide him, saying, "One can never tell what kind of a soul inhabits the body of any creature. So it is very important to be courteous and kind to all creatures on this earth."

58. THE SELF UNAWARE OF THE BODY

Sri Ramanasramam attracted all kinds of visitors. Human beings were only a part of the gathering around Bhagavan. The rest of the gathering consisted of cows, birds, dogs, monkeys, squirrels and other creatures. Sometimes these other 'visitors' enjoyed a much more intimate relationship with Bhagavan than any human being could hope for! Bhagavan's consideration for his animal-devotees, his concern for their welfare, his gentleness while dealing with animals, and his sympathy for them — all this could very well fill a human heart with envious longing! Sri Muruganar has mentioned this in his *Prarthanai Patthu*, wherein he sings, "Oh let me be born as a dog in Ramanasramam than to aspire for heavenly kingdom (*Sri Ramana Sannidhimurai*, v. 136)!"

In the early days of my stay at Arunachala, the temple elephant would pass the Ashram, on its way to the Arunachala Temple. The mahout would lead it in and the elephant would receive some food from the Ashram kitchen. Then it would go to greet Bhagavan with a loud trumpeting call and a salute, before proceeding on its trek to the temple.

Once, a youth from America was taking photographs of all the interesting spots in and around the Ashram. While he was walking around the grounds with his camera, he caught sight of Bhagavan and the temple elephant standing together near the Jubilee hall. Bhagavan was overseeing the feeding of the elephant, talking to it in gentle tones. The young American captured the moment on film. After a few days, he left the

Ashram and returned to America. Soon afterwards, he sent us a copy of the photograph he had taken. At the back of the photo, the young man had written, "A great body unaware of its soul, standing next to a great soul unaware of its body!" Nagammal wanted to know what the caption actually meant.

Bhagavan smiled at us and said, "You see, the elephant is so large that it has to have large quantities of food to sustain itself. Maybe the American boy feels that, in its preoccupation with trying to find enough food, the elephant cannot possibly find much time for soul-searching thoughts! So he says it is a great body which has not realised its soul. You have all seen how I stumble and struggle to walk straight. Perhaps that is why the boy says that I have no awareness of my body!'

A devotee remarked, "That is true. Bhagavan always appears to be totally unaware of his physical body." Bhagavan responded with a smile and the remark, "Various people say various things. One person says that I am like Lord Dakshinamoorthy. Another compares me to Lord Dandapani (Lord Subrahmanya) because I always have my staff (*dandam*) with me."

One of the devotees then said, "It is said that Jadabharata also had no awareness of his body. Is it because of this that he came to be known as Jadabharata?" Bhagavan replied, "Yes, of course! The ignorant might think that, the term 'Jadabharata' was applied to a man because he was inert and immobile, like an inanimate object. That is wrong. The real meaning of the word, in this context, is 'one who had no awareness of his physical body but established fully in the *atman*'."

* * *

I mentioned this incident to Sri Kunjuswami once. He was reminded of another incident. Bhagavan was rather unsteady on his feet, even in his younger days. His head and his body would shake, making it necessary for Bhagavan to use a cane to support himself. Once, when Sri Kunjuswami happened to find himself alone with Bhagavan, he asked, "Bhagavan, what causes your head and body to shake so much? Usually, such infirmities are seen only in the case of very old people. Why should Bhagavan be so afflicted at such a young age?" Bhagavan responded to this with a mischievous smile, saying, "What do you think would happen if you left a huge elephant tied up in a small hut? Would not the elephant's every movement make the fragile hut tremble and shake? That is what is happening here also." With this seemingly simple remark, Bhagavan had acknowledged the fact that his body was no more than a frail frame enclosing an unimaginably great spirit.

Bhagavan never seemed to be bothered by his physical infirmity. He joked about his own condition, saying, "All of you have only two legs each. I am the only one who has three legs!"

59. Bhagavan in Kitchen

Some of the spiritual seekers who had originally come to Tiruvannamalai to pursue their spiritual practices under the guidance of Bhagavan, through force of circumstances had to take up the kitchen responsibility. On the whole, these people were quite content with the situation, because they considered it a privilege to cook the food that Bhagavan partook of. However, they could not help feeling envious of those devotees who were fortunate enough to spend all their time in meditation in Bhagavan's presence, with easy access to his guidance and advice. At times, the kitchen staff felt quite frustrated at their confinement to the kitchen.

Bhagavan was aware of this. Being the very embodiment of compassion, he found a way to satisfy the longings of the kitchen staff. He made it a point to visit the kitchen on his way to the cowshed, and would often spend a fair amount of time talking to the cooks and helpers. He would give instructions and suggestions; at times, he would even assist the cooks in their work. Sometimes, Bhagavan would take a portion of some item and taste it. Then he would distribute a little of it among the others, and ask for their opinions. Oh what bliss to be offered something directly from the sacred hands of the Master!

Whenever something went wrong in the kitchen, Bhagavan would set it right. Once, the cooks were perplexed when they found that the dhal, in spite of boiling for an unusually long period, just could not be made soft enough to mash. (In South Indian cooking, dhal is an important ingredient of many dishes. For example, 'Sambar' requires that well-cooked dhal is added to the vegetables boiled in tamarind water.) Understandably, the cooks were becoming quite desperate because the delay in preparing the dhal would mean a delay in getting the meal ready. Bhagavan entered the kitchen just then. Taking in the situation, he said to the cook, "Add some salt to the dhal." The cook protested, saying, "Dhal only becomes harder if salt is added to it before it is fully cooked." Bhagavan did not waste any time in further talk. He simply scooped up a handful of salt from the container and sprinkled it over the boiling dhal. Within minutes, the dhal was a soft, mushy mixture, ready to be mixed with the other ingredients! Everyone was amazed because the common belief is that the addition of salt interferes with the process of cooking, and delays the softening up of dhal.

On another occasion, Bhagavan found that the 'Sambar' had too much salt in it. He instructed the cook to shape some cooked rice into a big ball, flatten it a little and drop it into the boiling hot Sambhar. Bhagavan told the kitchen staff that the rice would absorb the excess salt and the Sambhar was exceptionally delicious that day!

Varanasi Subbulakshmi used to say, "When you looked at Bhagavan reclining on the sofa in the meditation hall, surrounded by his devotees, you were reminded of Lord Krishna holding court in Mathura. While Bhagavan was in the kitchen, however, he was like Lord Krishna in Gokulam, sporting with the simple cowherd folk."

Bhagavan entered the kitchen very early in the morning while most of the devotees were still asleep, and completed the tasks like cutting the vegetables and grinding spices and chutneys. One morning, Bhagavan was preparing to grind the coconut chutney to be served with the iddlies at breakfast time. Anticipating Bhagavan's actions, Muruganar darted forward and took hold of the vertical stone that rotates within the cavity of the circular grinding stone. Muruganar started rotating the vertical stone, while Bhagavan settled down opposite and slowly pushed the coconut and other ingredients into the gap.

While this activity was going on, Bhagavan was talking about the early days. He said, "While we were staying on the Hill, Mother often remarked that a grinding stone would be a big help. I invariably replied that, once a grinding stone was acquired, some other appliance would appear indispensable, and there would be no end to such requirements. I used to tell Mother that, by acquiring one object after the other, we will only bind ourselves much more tightly to this earthly life."

Bhagavan's voice had a mesmeric effect upon Muruganar. Though his hands continued their mechanical activity, his mind was far away. He did not even notice that the chutney was ready; he just continued to rotate the stone. To catch his attention, Bhagavan splashed some water onto his face, under the pretext of sprinkling water over the chutney. Even then, Muruganar did not recognise the situation. He assumed that Bhagavan was sprinkling water on the ingredients, and some of the water had accidentally splashed into his eyes. So he just wiped his face with a towel, and continued with his activity. At that point, Bhagavan exclaimed, "What is this? Can't you see that the task is done? Why persist with the grinding when the chutney is ready?*" Only then did Muruganar realise what was happening.

Muruganar's devotion to Bhagavan was so total that, when Bhagavan was speaking, his attention got riveted upon Bhagavan's words, and he became oblivious to everything else around him. He had to be jolted back to reality by Bhagavan himself! Such incidents reveal the intimacy of the Master and the devotee. Is it not wonderful that Bhagavan should engage himself in such delightful sport with his devotees!

60. Vivekananda, I presume!

Bhagavan's presence was a haven of peace. Bhagavan would be reclining upon the sofa in the meditation hall, and devotees would be seated all around the sofa. For the most part, the entire gathering was perfectly silent. Only rarely did someone speak, for only rarely was the need for speech felt at all! Bhagavan and his disciples communed in the vibrant silence

---

* Sri Bhagavan aptly used the Tamil proverb அரைத்த மாவையே அரைக்கிறீர் which is used to denote a person who adamantly sticks to his own point of view.

which pervaded the meditation hall. Whenever Bhagavan's eyes fell upon us, we would feel electrified. All doubts would vanish and we would sink deep within ourselves. Our absorption in the Self was always enhanced by Bhagavan's Glance of Grace. We were like bees feeding upon the intoxicating nectar of Bhagavan's grace.

Once in a while, somebody would ask a question. Bhagavan seldom spoke, and even when he did, there was a great economy of words. In a few words, he could convey great meaning. One day a young, well educated man came to Bhagavan, prostrated and sat down. Somehow we got the impression that the youth was waiting for an opportunity to say something. The serene silence in the hall was soon broken by the young man's voice. He said to Bhagavan, "It is said that Ramakrishna Paramahamsa was able to elevate Vivekananda to the state of *Nirvikalpa Samadhi* with just a touch. Can Bhagavan do the same for me?" Bhagavan did not say anything. The young man waited, with obvious impatience, for Bhagavan's reply. After a few minutes of silence, Bhagavan looked at the youth and, in a soft voice, asked, "You are another Vivekananda, I presume?" The young man was taken aback. He was at a loss for words. His discomfiture was obvious to everyone in the hall. Clearly incapable of hiding his embarrassment, the young man got up and left the hall without another word!

After the young man had left the place, Bhagavan remarked to us, "Nobody appreciates the need for self-analysis and self-criticism. The general tendency is to think of oneself as perfect, and to look for opportunities to cast aspersions on the nature of all other people. This boy has no time to examine his own nature. All he could see was this Sadhu reclining on a sofa, surrounded by a group of reverant disciples. He wanted to see whether I was really worthy of all this reverence. So he took it upon himself to challenge me! Though he was eager to see whether I had the power of Sri Ramakrishna, he was not bothered about whether he himself merited comparison with Vivekananda. That is because he assumed that he himself was perfect. If he had paused to think about his own worthiness, he would never have asked such a question. Sri Ramakrishna bestowed that rare state upon Vivekananda alone, because Vivekananda was a person of rare spiritual merit. To one who is engaged in self-enquiry, all other questions become irrelevant and unimportant."

The young man who had initiated this discussion could not derive much benefit, because he had already left the place. But Bhagavan's words had a profound effect upon all of us in the hall. Bhagavan often told us that the only way to keep the mind from indulging in criticism of others, would be to turn the mind inwards and engage it in self-examination.

Similarly, some people used to study the scriptures and come to Bhagavan with doubts about seemingly contradictory statements made therein. They not only asked for an explanation of the contradiction, but also wanted to know the purpose behind making such confusing statements!

Bhagavan would listen to such queries with patience, and reply, "Whose is this doubt about the seeming contradictions? Is it the author of the scripture who is confused, or is the confusion in your own mind? Those who made the statements can take the responsibility of validating those statements. Why should you worry about that? Try to understand yourself first. When you get to know your Self, you will see that you know everything else, as well. As long as you are not sure of your Self, how can you understand the minds of those who wrote the scriptures?"

61. The Golden Parrot

The Sri Matrubhuteswara temple was nearing completion. All the preparations for the consecration ceremony were going on at full speed. The temple was being given finishing touches, and materials were being gathered for the various *Homams* and other religious ceremonies. To co-ordinate the various activities connected with the consecration ceremony, a committee was formed. Prof. T.K.Duraiswami Iyer was one of the members of this committee. He discharged his duties with great sincerity and devotion.

Duraiswami Iyer and his wife Yogambal, were regular visitors to the Ashram. They had rented a house in Tiruvannamalai town, and they came to the Ashram every morning and evening, and spent a lot of time in meditation, in Bhagavan's presence. Yogambal was a devotee of the Mother Goddess. She would often invite Bhagavan's devotees to her house, and talk to them about their experiences in Bhagavan's presence. She was a very generous lady and she never hesitated to help those in need. Their house was always full of guests.

Yogambal had one fond wish. She wanted to have a small golden parrot made, and place it in the hand of the Goddess in the Matrubhuteswara temple. So, Duraiswami Iyer commissioned a jeweller to make a golden parrot of a suitable size. The golden parrot was made and delivered to Duraiswami Iyer in due time. That evening, when the couple made their customary visit to the Ashram, Yogambal had the golden figure in her hand. After prostrating to Bhagavan, she gave the golden parrot to Bhagavan and said, "This parrot has been made with the idea of placing it in the Goddess' hand." Bhagavan took the small figure in his hand and, turning it this way and that, admired the delicate craftsmanship. Bhagavan then smiled at the couple and said, "This is a parrot suitable for the Goddess to hold in Her hand. What a wonderful coincidence! The one who is offering the parrot is Yogambal and the one who is receiving it is Yogambal too!" The deity in the Matrubhuteswara Temple is named Yogambal. By remarking upon this coincidence, the lady was moved to tears.

62. WHAT CAN YOU DO ABOUT THIS?

Once, a Westerner who was on a visit to the Ashram, brought a folding canvas chair to the meditation hall. Not being used to sitting on the floor, he had obviously hit upon the idea of using this low chair to enable him to meditate in Bhagavan's presence. As the visitor was unfolding the chair and setting it up, an Ashram attendant noticed what was going on. The attendant approached the visitor and told him that it was not the practice to sit on a raised seat in Bhagavan's presence. The visitor felt that it was impossible for him to sit on the floor, so he picked up his chair and left the hall.

Bhagavan was watching this and told the attendant, "So! You have done a great service to your Master, have you not? That man was planning to use a chair because he could not sit on the floor. You very cleverly prevented him from acting in such a disrespectful fashion. Now what are you planning to do about this other person who is sitting right above my head?" All of us looked up, and saw a big monkey perched on the roof of the hall, directly above Bhagavan's head. Until Bhagavan pointed out the monkey, nobody had noticed it. Now all our eyes were upon it; but the monkey was totally unconcerned about the attention it was receiving from the people below.

Bhagavan said, "If at all we are able to do it, we try to impose our will upon others. If the other person happens to be stronger, we let him have his way. That is human nature. Why should we concern ourselves with such trivial matters? What difference can it make, whether a person sits on the floor or upon a chair? What is high and what is low? Are these not mere concepts? Should we not learn to look beyond these things?"

63. THE MARAUDING MONKEYS

While Bhagavan was staying in the Jubilee Hall, all his animal devotees had the maximum degree of freedom. Monkeys, squirrels, peacocks, dogs and cows — all of them could come and go as they pleased. Each creature was assured of an affectionate welcome from Bhagavan and he knew all about them. He would make enquiries about their welfare and would ply them with tasty tidbits. He was aware of their personal preferences and would make sure that each got his favourite snacks! Some of the peacocks had a preference for cashew nuts, and would refuse to eat puffed rice. Bhagavan would instruct his attendant to get the nuts from the container and he would feed them with his own hands.

Of all the animals, the monkeys were the boldest. They are mischievous and clever by nature. The Ashram monkeys enjoyed the special privilege of Bhagavan's indulgent affection, and you will understand why the monkeys were able to get away with the most outrageous escapades! Visitors to the Ashram would bring fruits, sweets and other eatables as offerings to Bhagavan. Many an unwary visitor was pounced upon by the monkeys, and robbed of the delicacies meant to be offerred to

Bhagavan. As the devotees and the attendants watched helplessly, Bhagavan would smile mischievously, as if to say, "You are no match for my monkey friends!"

Whenever a devotee brought fruits as an offering to Bhagavan, the fruits would be placed on a stool in front of Bhagavan's sofa. The attendant would put them away safely in a basket. One day, a devotee brought a variety of fruits. This was his first visit to the Ashram and so he did not know about the monkeys. He spread all the fruits on a large tray and was approaching the hall with the tray in his hands when a bold little monkey leapt upon the tray, grabbed a handful of fruits and disappeared into the branches of a tree. This caused quite a commotion, with some people trying to catch the fleeing monkey, and others concentrating upon shooing off other potential 'robbers'! Bhagavan heard the noise and looked out. When he saw the clever little monkey running off with his booty, Bhagavan burst into laughter. In amused tones, he remarked, "The monkeys obviously know that they might not get any of the fruits, once the tray is brought into the hall. So they must have decided to take their due share while they still had the chance! Now that the monkeys have taken matters into their own hands, what are you going to do?"

Once, a devotee brought some fruits to the hall. He placed the fruits on the stool, prostrated to Bhagavan and went and sat down with the other devotees. The attendant was not in the room at the time and the fruits remained upon the stool. A small monkey, standing near the screen behind Bhagavan's sofa, was gazing at the fruits with longing in its eyes. It must have been a rather timid monkey, as it hesitated to come forward and snatch up the fruits. Bhagavan saw the little fellow and gave an encouraging nod. As though it had been waiting just for this encouragement, the monkey darted forward, grabbed some fruits and scrambled up to the thatched roof of the hall. Perched there, safely out of human reach, the monkey was happily feasting on the fruits when the attendant returned to the hall. As soon as the attendant entered the hall, Bhagavan said, "You must thank him for doing you a favour." The attendant was puzzled by Bhagavan's remark. Bhagavan explained: "Somebody brought some fruits. You were not here at the time. Seeing that your job had to be done, he decided to take care of it himself." Saying this, Bhagavan pointed to the monkey on the roof. Then he added, "There is a small difference in the way the two of you go about the job, however! Whereas you would have put the fruits in a basket, he chose to put them in his stomach! Anyway, he has disposed of the fruits and for that, you should thank him."

One evening, a female monkey entered the hall. A baby was hugging her belly. The monkey approached the basket of fruits beside Bhagavan's sofa. The attendant tried to drive her away. Bhagavan chided the attendant, saying, "She is a mother with a child to feed. Can you not spare a few fruits for her?" But the attendant did not heed Bhagavan's words. Frightened by his threatening gestures, the monkey ran away and climbed up a tree. Bhagavan said to his attendant, "This is all we are capable of! We talk about our reverence for those who have renounced the world. We seek out Sannyasins and worship them. But when a true Sannyasin comes to us, we drive him away. What does a monkey care for worldly wealth? We humans store food in rooms with strong doors, with a lock. What do these monkeys do? They eat whatever they can get, and take shelter on some tree at night. Do they save for the future? They do not even develop attachment to their own children. As long as the baby is too young to take care of itself, the mother carries it around wherever she goes.

Once the baby is old enough to fend for itself, she just sets him down and lets him go his own way. We are the ones who cling to property and worldly ties. Tell me, who is the real *sannyasin*, the monkey or the people here? Moreover, this monkey is a female and therefore, timid by nature. A male monkey might fight for his rights and snatch away whatever he could, but a female just gives in meekly." Bhagavan then looked at the monkey and beckoned her in soft and gentle tones. The monkey approached and stood before Bhagavan's sofa. He gave it some fruits and the monkey went away happy.

Once, a group of young monkeys entered the hall. When chased, they went straight to Bhagavan and scrambled under his sofa, as though they knew that nobody could touch them as long as they stayed close to Bhagavan! The attendants hesitated to chase them, as they had found shelter under Bhagavan's sofa. The monkeys took full advantage of the situation and went so far as to make faces at the attendants. Bhagavan was amused, and he made it clear that he was on the monkeys' side, by rewarding the cheeky little creatures with fruits and nuts!

64. God Alone Exists

Those who have realised the Self, even when they are engaged in everyday activities, remain uninvolved. They are always in a state of utter stillness. Bhagavan himself has described this, in the thirtieth verse of the *Supplement to Reality in Forty Verses*.

"The mind that is devoid of attachments, though it may appear to be engaged in activity, is in reality inactive — just like the mind of a person listening to a story, might wander off to a faraway place".

Once, we were all listening to the radio, in the Jubilee hall. At the end of the program, the names of all the artistes were announced. Bhagavan said, "See! The radio sings and gives speeches. It even announces the names of the performers. But there is nobody inside the radio. Our existence is also like that. The body might appear to walk and talk and perform a number of functions. But in fact, there is no individual inside the body. Everything is God. He alone exists." Bhagavan continued, "The concepts of time and space are also imaginary. When we listen to a concert on the radio, are we bothered about the exact time and location at which the concert took place? What difference can it make to our enjoyment of the music? Whether the concert took place in Hyderabad or in Madras, we can listen to the music and derive the same degree of enjoyment, sitting right here in this hall.

The wise one does not attach any importance to concepts of space and time. One has to go through certain situations in a given lifetime and for this, a body is required. That is the only reason for acquiring a body. He goes through various experiences, without getting involved in anything. To an ordinary person, worldly experiences seem real. An ordinary man might think that a liberated person has all the experiences that others have. But the liberated person has no attachment to the body and therefore, physical experiences hold no significance for him.

The *jivanmukta* has the same attitude towards his body that a railway porter has for the luggage he carries. Just as the porter carries the luggage upto the stipulated spot and lays it down at that spot, the *jivanmukta* carries the body through the pre-ordained experiences of a lifetime and, at the end of the course, he lays down the burden with relief. The porter thinks of the load on his head only as a burden; he does not identify with it on a personal level. That is why he feels no regret when he puts it down. It is the same in the case of a *jivanmukta*. As he never thinks of the body as having any personal significance, he feels no sorrow when the time comes for him to leave the body."

During the last days of Bhagavan's earthly life, when his devotees beseeched him to retain the human form for a long time, Bhagavan used to say, "A *jnani* (a realised soul) knows that the sole purpose of acquiring a body is to enable the spirit to attain knowledge through experiences. Do we feel sad because we have to throw away the used leaf-plate after a meal? In the same way, a *jnani* discards the human body without any regret or sorrow."

65. The Brinjal Stalks

Once, a devotee sent a sackful of brinjals to the Ashram. After making a variety of tasty dishes, the remaining brinjals were sun-dried and preserved for later use. The discarded stalks were piled up in a heap in a corner of the kitchen. When Bhagavan saw the heap of brinjal stalks, he said, "Why have the stalks been thrown away? They can be cooked and served as one of the dishes during a meal." One of the kitchen attendants exclaimed, "Bhagavan! How can anybody eat brinjal stalks! The stalks are not edible!"

Bhagavan did not reply but took up a knife and started working on the heap of stalks. He removed the outer fibrous sheath and exposed the tender portion within and proceeded to chop this soft core into tiny pieces. The attendants followed Bhagavan's instructions and set to work on the stalks. Soon, they had a basket full of finely chopped brinjal stalks. Early the next morning, Bhagavan entered the kitchen and showed the cook how to cook the brinjal stalks. Bhagavan directed the cook to put a large frying pan on the stove and to fry the chopped pieces in hot oil. The fried brinjal stalk was then mixed with the broken rice which was boiling in a large vessel. When the mixture of brinjal stalk and broken rice had been cooked well, the seasoning was added and the *uppuma* for that day's breakfast was ready. Everybody found the breakfast tasty that morning.

After having his breakfast, Bhagavan went to the hall. As it was a Sunday, Sub-Registrar Narayana Iyer was in the Ashram that day. When Bhagavan saw Narayana Iyer, he made the usual enquiries about his welfare and then asked, "Did you have breakfast this morning?" Narayana Iyer replied, "Yes. I had uppuma." Bhagavan asked, "Did you notice anything special about today's uppuma?" Narayana Iyer said, "Yes. It was particularly tasty today. It had a special flavour. I think cabbage had been added to the other ingredients and that gave the *uppuma* that special flavour." Bhagavan chuckled, "Cabbage? It was chopped brinjal stalk that you ate!" Everyone present was amazed when they heard this. Whoever could have guessed that brinjal stalks could taste so good! Narayana Iyer voiced the belief of all the devotees by saying, "The touch of Bhagavan's hands must have imparted the unique flavour to the dish. The Grace of Bhagavan can transform the most unlikely ingredients into a dish fit for the Gods!"

Bhagavan never tolerated wastage. The vegetable peelings and other items which could not be consumed by humans, were to be fed to the birds and the animals which frequented the Ashram. Nothing was to be thrown away. Bhagavan's frugal nature was obvious in everything he handled. Bhagavan took great care to put paper, pencils, cardboard and other items to optimum use. The methods he adopted, to avoid wastage, never ceased to amaze and impress his devotees.

* * *

Once, plantain flowers were being prepared for use in some dish. The outer red skin of the plantain flower is rather tough and is considered inedible. These skins had been removed and thrown into the waste-basket. Bhagavan was on his way to the cowshed when he saw the pile of discarded skins. He remarked to the attendant who was accompanying him, "Look! They have thrown out the portion which is richest in nutritive content. What a waste!" Bhagavan's attendant was intrigued by these words. He asked, "Bhagavan! What nutritive value can there be, in the skin of plantain flowers?" Bhagavan replied, "The red outer covering of the plantain flower is rich in fat. See how the inner side of the skin glistens! Ascetics eat this skin so that their body can get the fat required for proper nourishment. Ascetics cannot consume ghee and butter, can they? The skin of plantain flowers can be used as a good source of fat. An additional advantage is that this fat actually helps in developing the capacity for controlling the senses." The attendant recounted this interesting conversation to the Ashram cooks. They were curious about the method of cooking the skin of plantain flowers.

By coincidence, someone brought a large quantity of plantain flowers to the Ashram, within a few days. The kitchen attendants requested Bhagavan to show them how to cook the red outer skin covering of the flowers. Bhagavan said, "Soak some red gram (thoor dhal) in water. Clean the skins and chop them finely. Grind the soaked gram, along with salt, red chillies and asafoetida. Add the chopped skin to this paste, and steam the mixture for a few minutes. When the mixture is cooked, remove it from the fire and allow it to cool. Then crumble it and roast the crumbled mixture in hot oil. Season it with mustard seeds, and the dish is ready. This preparation can be used as a side dish with rice."

The cooks prepared the dish as per Bhagavan's instructions. Everybody found the preparation very tasty, and many remarked upon the subtle flavour. The cooks were very happy. However, the next time plantain flowers were brought to the Ashram, the cooks felt reluctant to repeat the laborious process of preparation. So, they dug a pit and buried the plantain flower skins at a spot which they thought Bhagavan would not visit. The next morning, when Bhagavan was returning from the cowshed, he saw a wounded dog by the side of the path. He approached the dog and attended to its wounds. After comforting the dog, Bhagavan was about to get back to the path when he noticed the mound of earth. He poked at the mound with his walking stick and soon the plantain flower skins lay exposed. How can anything be hidden from his all-seeing eyes! The kitchen attendants waited apprehensively for Bhagavan's reprimand. But Bhagavan merely said, "If you felt that the preparation of these skins would be too difficult, you could have fed it to the cows. Why bury the skins in the mud? What a waste of good stuff!" O.K. Do what you like? Why should I bother?

Bhagavan would sometimes tell us what to do. But he never forced us to follow his instructions. It was up to us to absorb his teachings and to benefit from the lessons he taught us.

66. ABSOLUTE PERFECTION

It was a festival day, and *modakams* were being prepared in the Ashram kitchen. (*modakam* is a sweet prepared in South India, as an offering to Lord Ganesa).

On that particular day, Shanthamma, Sam*poornam*ma, Shankaramma, Lokamma and some others were engaged in making the *modakams*. Each of them had a portion of *poornam* (jaggery and coconut mixture) in a plate, and they were moulding the rice flour into cups and filling the cups with *poornam*. Each of the ladies worked at her own pace and so, some of them finished their portion of the *poornam* faster than the others.

On his way to the cowshed, Bhagavan entered the kitchen and stood for a few moments, watching the ladies at their work. The conversation among the ladies included remarks like, 'My *poornam* is over. You have so much *poornam* with you. Why don't you give me some of your *poornam?*'and, 'Oh! You don't have any *poornam* left. Why don't you take some of mine?' and 'I have very little *poornam* left. Please give me some more, etc.' After a while, one of the ladies got up, saying, 'All my *poornam* is over.'

Bhagavan, who had been listening to the ladies' remarks, smiled at them and said, "You have all been talking about *poornam*. One of you said you had too little *poornam* and another said she could spare a little of her *poornam*. One lady even remarked that all her *poornam* was over. Whatever the context in which it was used, the word retained its meaning. Whether there was too much *poornam* or too little *poornam* or no *poornam* at all, the identity of *poornam* (Wholeness) remained unchanged. This unchanging nature is the mark of everlasting perfection. The ideal of absolute perfection is set out in the benedictory verse of the *Isavasasya Upanishad* thus: "That is the Whole. This is also the Whole. The Whole comes out of the Whole. When you remove the Whole from the Whole, what remains is also Whole."*

This verse tells us about the nature of the Universe and its Creator. The Self remains unchanged, both when It is in its unmanifest state, and when It manifests Itself as the universe and

---

* *Om Poornamadah, Poornamidam, Poornat Poornamudachyate, Poornasya Poornamadaya Poornameva Vashishyate.*

the creations therein. That which separates itself from the Absolute, and manifests itself as the universe, is also perfect and whole. That from which the universe is created, is also unchanging, immutable and everlasting perfection. Paradoxical though this might sound, great sages have found this to be the Truth.

It is this beautiful philosophical idea that Bhagavan expounded to the ladies in the Ashram kitchen. By relating philosophical ideas to everyday incidents, Bhagavan made it possible for simple people to grasp the most complex ideas.

67. NAMMALVAR

Nammalvar enjoys a special place among the spiritual leaders of the *Vaishnavite* sect. The *Vaishnavite* leaders are traditionally classified into two categories viz., *Alwars* and *Acharyas*. Nammalvar enjoys the unique distinction of being considered an *Alwar* as well as an *Acharya*. All other *Vaishnavite* saints are regarded as the various limbs of the great Body of *Vaishnavism*, whereas Nammalvar is said to be the Spirit that enlivens the Body.

If we study the hierarchy of *Vaishnavite* spiritual leaders, we can see that the first three of them had no earthly existence; they were supernatural beings inhabiting a world beyond ours. Nammalvar was the first of the saints to assume a human form. He is the fourth in the line of Vaishnavite saints, and Ramanuja is the tenth.

Nammalvar was born, in a small village called Alwartirunagari, in the ninth century AD. Nammalvar's parents, Kaariyar and his wife Udaya Nangai, belonged to the Velala (farmer) community. The couple was childless, and prayed to the Lord of Tirukkurungudi to blees them with a child.

It is said that Nammalvar was an incarnation of Vishvaksena, one of the celestial beings in Lord Vishnu's retinue. When the child was born, his parents named him Maran. In later life, he came to be known by ten different names, including Sadagopan, Tirukkurugoor Nambi and Parankusan. As an infant, Nammalvar never drank mother's milk, never cried and lay inert all the time. In spite of all these peculiarities, however, the baby was quite healthy. Perturbed by their infant son's unusual characterestics, the parents took him to the temple and left him there. Lord Vishnu commanded His attendant Vishvaksena to go and give spiritual initiation to the infant Nammalvar. As soon as he received initiation, Nammalvar went and sat under the tamarind tree in the temple compound, and immersed himself in meditation for sixteen years. It is said that the celestial serpent Adisesha had taken the form of a tamarind tree in order to provide shelter for the saint.

During this period, Madurakavi, a *brahmin* belonging to a village called Tirukkolur in the Pandya kingdom, went on a pilgrimage to North India. While he was in Ayodhya, he became aware of a wonderful light on the Southern horizon. Fascinated by this mysterious light, Madurakavi decided to trace it to its source. The light apppeared only during the nights, and could not be seen in the daytime. He followed this light through the Godavari region, Tiruvengadam and Srirangam. Eventually, he reached Alwartirunagari. The light disappeared into the temple there. He questioned the local people and came to know about Nammalvar's birth and the details of his life.

Madurakavi entered the temple and approached the tamarind tree under which Nammalvar was seated and instantly knew that he must be an extraordinary person. Desirous of speaking to the saint, he went close to him and clapped his hands loudly. The noise roused Nammalvar from his contemplation, and he opened his eyes. Madurakavi immediately asked, "If the Small One issues from the womb of the Cosmos, what would it eat, and where would it rest? (சித்தின் வயிற்றில் சிறியது பிறந்தால் எத்தைத் தின்று எங்கே கிடக்கும்?)" The actual meaning of this rather cryptic question is: "If the individual soul issues from the Cosmic Absolute, how would it sustain itself, and where would it find shelter?"

Nammalvar replied without the least hesitation, "It would feed upon That, and would reside within That." This means, "The individual soul will continue to draw sustenance from That (the Absolute Reality) and would ever reside within That (அத்தைத் தின்று அங்கே கிடக்கும்)." In other words, the individual soul continues to be the Absolute, and does not really have a separate identity of its own.

These were the first words Nammalvar had uttered. It was Madurakavi's good fortune that Nammalvar's very first words should serve as a valuable lesson in spirituality. When he heard these words, he was overcome by emotion. He fell at Nammalvar's feet and said, "Master, I surrender myself to you. May it please you to make use of your humble servant." Nammalvar accepted him as his disciple and said, "I shall compose some songs which will transport all listeners to the Abode of God. It shall be your duty to record these songs on silk fabric."

Nammalvar then proceeded to sing the *Tiruvrittam*, the *Tiruvasiriyam*, the *Periya Tiruvandadi* and the *Tiruvaimozhi*. These four Tamil compositions are considered to be on par with the four *Vedas* for *Vaishnavites*, and Nammalvar is therefore revered as the one who gave the Tamil speaking world its own *Vedas*. The most sacred book of the *Vaishnavites* is the *Nalayira Divya Prabhandam*, and it contains 1296 songs composed by Nammalvar. All of Nammalvar's compositions were written down by Madurakavi.

Madurakavi, in adddition to recording all his Master's compositions, was responsible for some compositions of his own. The remarkable fact about Madurakavi is that, whereas all other *Vaishnavite* saints sang the praises of Lord Vishnu, Madurakavi sang about the greatness of his spiritual Master (Nammalvar) alone. In all, Madurakavi has composed eleven beautiful songs in praise of his Guru. These poems are of such remarkable sweetness that the disciple came to be called Madurakavi.

Once, while in the Jubilee Hall, Bhagavan was talking about how the *Reality in Forty Verses* came to be composed. T.K.Sundaresa Iyer asked Bhagavan, "In the *Reality in Forty Verses*, the word *Ulladu* has been used in the context of the Reality, or the Self. Has this particular word been used in the same way by anyone else?" Bhagavan replied, "That which does not exist, cannot make an appearance." After a short pause, Bhagavan added, "This particular usage can be seen in Nammalvar's songs." Then Bhagavan asked Venkataratnam to bring the relevant book and read aloud some of the passages. These passages include the 9th stanza of the *Tiruvaimozhi*, etc. In every one of these soings, the word *Ulladu* has been used in exactly the same sense that Bhagavan has used it. Bhagavan continued, "Staunch *Vaishnavites* seldom quote from Nammalvar's works. This is because many of his works are *Advaitic* in nature and so, *Vaishnavites* find it difficult to find support for their theories in Nammalvar's works. In fact, it is said that *Vaishnavites* often remark that Nammalvar has played a rather cruel trick on them (நம்மைக் கெடுத்தான் நம்மாழ்வான்)!" During the course of his conversations, Bhagavan often referred to Nammalvar 's poems. Muruganar, too, made frequent references to Nammalvar 's works and often remarked upon the similarities between Nammalvar 's statements and Bhagavan's teachings.

68. SWAMI PRANAVANANDA

Swami Pranavananda was one of the earliest devotees to come to Bhagavan. He visited Bhagavan in 1910, in the Virupaksha Cave. His integrity and strong spiritual aspirations earned him an enviable place among Bhagavan's devotees. He was one of Bhagavan's intimate companions. His love for Bhagavan was so great that he surrendered himself unconditionally at Bhagavan's feet, relinquishing all worldly attachments, and this filled his heart with joy and peace. He was very modest and never spoke about himself and his speech was restricted to the barest minimum. Though he did not consider himself a teacher, his life itself served as a valuable lesson in spirituality. Pranavananda belonged to the Sarvepalli family, which was highly esteemed in the village of Venkatapuram, near Tiruttani in South India. The Sarvepalli family was a stronghold of learning in the *Vedas*, *sastras* and *puranas*. The family deity was Lord Yoganarasimha of Sholingapuram, and Pranavananda was named Narasimham after the family deity. He took the name of Swami Pranavananda at the time of becoming a *sannyasi*.

Dr. Sarvepalli Radhakrishnan, the world famous philosopher and one of the most illustrious Presidents of India, was Narasimham's nephew. Surprisingly enough, Dr. Radhakrishnan, who is esteemed for his erudition and wisdom, was rather dull as a child. His father was very much upset by Radhakrishnan's nature, and concerned about his future. Narasimham offered to take the boy to Vellore and take care of his education. Upon reaching Vellore, Narasimham initiated his nephew in the Ramataraka Mantram. Constant repetition of this potent Mantram resulted in the blossoming of

Radhakrishnan's intellect and he grew into a brilliant student. He joined the Uris College in Vellore and passed his Intermediate course. By taking care of Radhakrishnan during the formative years of his life, and by helping him through the initial stages of his academic career, Narasimham can be said to have laid the foundation for Radhakrishnan's success in later life.

The Sarvepalli family was not a wealthy one. It is said that though Goddess Saraswati (the Goddess of Learning) showered Her Grace upon the family, Goddess Lakshmi (the Goddess of Wealth) looked askance at them! Though they were never reduced to extreme poverty, the family never enjoyed the comforts of affluence. With the intention of acqiring some wealth, some members of the Sarvepalli family migrated to Madras, where they were able to make some money by giving discourses in sastras and puranas. Later on, some of the members settled down in Tiruttani. Narasimham was well versed in the three South Indian languages namely Telugu, Tamil and Kannada. He was also a Sanskrit scholar. Ironically enough, Narasimham did not get through the Matriculation Examination, but his scholarship in English was remarkable. Englishmen themselves used to marvel at his mastery over the language!

Narasimham joined the Arcot Christian College as a teacher. The authorities were so impressed by his scholarship and his capacity as a teacher that they appointed him as a Munshi (a teacher who trained foreigners in the use of local languages) to teach Telugu and English to the members of the mission and the managers of the institutions under their care.

Narasimham also trained some of the members of the mission in the techniques of meditation. Some of his students, like Paul Adiseshayya and Ida Scudder (who founded the CMC Hospital in Vellore) were so impressed by the clarity of thought obtained through meditation that they were prepared to embrace Hinduism if Narasimham advised them to do so. Narasimham did not believe in religious conversions, and did not think that only Hindus could benefit from meditation. He declared that one could meditate on God even if one did not profess any religion. He told his students that one could serve mankind and live in peace even if one did not belong to any recognised religion. Narasimham's beliefs and his teachings astonished the authorities of the mission.

Narasimham made several visits to the Vellore Central Jail, to meet the prisoners and to talk to them about moral values. He initiated the prisoners into the Ramataraka mantram and persuaded them to give up their lawless ways. Through his influence, Narasimham helped in reforming and rehabilitating many of the criminals in the jail. He left the Mission because of some difference of opinion with the authorities, and took up the job of Munshi in the Police Training College. Many of the Europeans who came to Vellore during that period had the good fortune to learn the local language from Narasimham. Those who were spiritually inclined found an able guide in him, and his classes became very popular *satsangs* (spiritual congregations). Very soon, Narasimham gained the reputation of a capable teacher and a spiritual guide.

While Narasimham was serving as a Munshi in Vellore, Kavyakanta Ganapati Muni was working as a Telugu Teacher in the same town. In 1910, Narasimham and Ganapati Muni went to Tiruvannamalai and met Bhagavan. At that time, Bhagavan was staying in the Virupaksha Cave. In the very first meeting, Bhagavan's look of grace entered deep into

Narasimham's heart and destroyed all the doubts that had been troubling him till then. From that moment onwards, Narasimham's heart was full of peace. It was during this period that F.H.Humphreys came to India as as Assistant Superintendent of Police. As soon as he reached Bombay, he fell ill, and had to be hospitalised. Upon being discharged from the hospital, he came to Vellore. He reached Vellore on March 18th, and Narasimham went to him on the same day, to start the Telugu classes. As soon as he saw Narasimham, Humphreys asked him whether he knew any astrology. Narasimham said he did not. Humphreys then requested Narasimham to get him a particular book on astrology. Narasimham obtained the book from the local library.

The next day, while returning the book, Humphreys asked Narasimham whether he knew any *mahatmas* (great souls) in Vellore. Narasimham did not feel like divulging any such information to an inquisitive foreigner and so he said that he did not know anyone. At their next meeting, Humphreys said, "Why, Munshiji! You told me you did not know any *mahatmas* in this town. But last night I saw your guru in my dream. He was sitting beside me and saying something, but I could not understand him. You were the first person I saw in my dream while I was in Bombay, and I felt that you would lead me to my guru."

Narasimham replied, "I have never travelled beyond Guntakal. I never went to Bombay." Humphreys then gave a detailed description of the vision he had had while lying in the hospital in Bombay. He said that even as he lay upon the hospital bed in Bombay, he had gone to Vellore in his astral body. He had seen some people in Vellore, and Narasimham was the first person he saw. Narasimham was impressed by the yogic powers of his new student, but he wanted to test him further.

When Narasimham came to teach Humphreys that afternoon, he brought some pictures of Bhagavan, Ganapati Muni, Seshadri Swami and some others. He put these pictures on the table and, without meeting Humphreys or giving him any kind of explanation, he went to teach another student. When Narasimham returned, Humphreys was waiting for him eagerly. Holding out Ganapati Muni's picture, Humphreys said, "This is the person I saw in my dream yesterday. Is he not your guru? Please tell me the truth." Narasimham was amazed, and he admitted that it was indeed the picture of his guru, Sri Ganapati Muni. Narasimham had become Ganapati Muni's disciple in 1906, and the Muni had explained Bhagavan's teachings, and trained him in the method of Self-enquiry as taught by Bhagavan.

A fortnight later, Humphreys fell ill again. He was sent to Udagamandalam (Ooty), to recuperate. While in Ooty, Humphreys kept up a regular correspondence with Narasimham. After returning from Udagamandalam, Humphreys sketched the picture of a cave with a mountain spring at its entrance, and a Muni standing in front of the cave. He showed the picture to Narasimham and told him that it was the representation of what he had seen in his dream the previous night. Humphreys asked Narasimham whether he could identify the sage in the picture. Narasimham was amazed to see that Humphreys had drawn a picture of Ramana Maharshi standing in front of the Virupaksha Cave. When he was told about this, Humphreys expressed the desire to meet Bhagavan.

Humphreys had been asking Narasimham to take him to meet Ganapati Muni. It so happened that Ganapati Muni came to Vellore around that time. The Muni was on his way to Tiruvannamalai, and had stopped in Vellore because he had been invited to give a discourse in the Theosophical Society there. While he was in Vellore, Narasimham took Humphreys to meet him. When the Muni resumed his journey to Tiruvannamalai, Humphreys took a day's leave from work, and accompanied the Muni and Narasimham to Tiruvannamalai. Thus it was that Humphreys had his first darshan of Bhagavan in the Virupaksha Cave, in the year 1911, and Narasimham was instrumental in bringing about this momentous meeting.

While he was teaching Telugu to the officials in the Police Department, Narasimham used to translate several spiritual texts, including the Ramayana, for the benefit of his students. The Englishmen were highly impressed by Narasimham's mastery of their language, and his lucid style. They held him in high regard, both for his scholarship and for his spiritual achievements.

Most of Narasimham's students were very wealthy people, in important, influential positions. But Narasimham treated all his students equally, without fear or favour. He made no demands, but the Englishmen used to send a motor buggy to pick him up from his house and to drop him back after classes. The chauffeur used to salute Narasimham as though he were the Governor! Very rarely was such reverence shown to an Indian during the days of the British Raj. Though he was just a teacher of local languages, Narasimham commanded the respect of a large number of foreigners.

Though Narasimham had originally accepted Ganapati Muni as his *guru*, he was proud to declare himself a devotee of Bhagavan Ramana. He led a very simple life; but he never hesitated to help those in need. Though his was a very modest house in a crowded street (named Avalkaran Veedhi), there were at least ten students staying with him at any given time. He boarded them free of charge, and his wife fed them all with the loving concern of a mother.

Narasimham had no male issue. This fact did not bother him, but his wife longed for a son. One day, she requested Ganapati Muni to bless her with a male child. With the Muni's blessings, a baby boy was born, but he did not survive beyond early childhood.

Narasimham's wife was an ardent devotee of Lord Yoganarasimha of Sholingapuram, and she often visited His temple on the Ghatikachalam hill. Late one evening, while she was sitting in meditation behind the idols of the Saptha Rishis (Seven Sages) the temple priests, who had not noticed her, locked up the temple for the night and went home. The lady claimed that, on that occasion, Lord Yoganarasimha Himself brought her out of the locked temple and sat her on the steps leading up the hill.

Narasimham had no special feeling towards his family deity, Lord Yoganarasimha. His whole concentration was on the Vichara Marga (path of Self-enquiry) as taught by Bhagavan. In course of time, Narasimham renounced the world and became a Sannyasi, assuming the name of Swami Pranavananda. However, the ritual was a mere formality, as Narasimham had always been a Sannyasi at heart, living a life of detachment and devoting his time to spiritual pursuits.

Pranavananda considered Bhagavan the very personification of the *Vedas* and the *Upanishads*, and so he had great love and reverence for him. Bhagavan, too, had a special regard and concern for Pranavananda. The following anecdote serves as an illustration of Bhagavan's concern for him: Pranavananda used to compile Bhagavan's teachings into books. One of the devotees owned a printing press, and he printed the books that were brought to him by Pranavananda. One hot summer afternoon, Pranavananda was returning to Tiruvannamalai with a copy of one of the books. He had just one rupee with him, and, not wanting to engage a bullock cart, he decided to walk to Ramanasramam. He somehow made it to the gate of the ashram, but the terrible heat had taken its toll; Pranavananda could not proceed any further. He sat down in the shade of a tree for a short rest before entering the ashram. At that moment, Bhagavan happened to look out of the window. Seeing Pranavananda's exhausted attitude, Bhagavan immediately came out to him. Sitting down beside him, Bhagavan poured cool water over Pranavananda's sore feet and spoke to him in gentle, compassionate tones, saying, "Why do you put yourself to such strain? Did I ever ask you to go out in this heat?" Such was the Master's concern for his disciple's welfare!

Pranavanada was instrumental in printing several books of Bhagavan's teachings. He priced these books at half-anna or one anna and gave them to the ashram. It was his desire that Bhagavan's teachings should be made available to the maximum number of people at affordable cost. It was Pranavananada who first translated Bhagavan's *Who am I?*, *Vicharasangraham*, *Vivekachudamani* and *Devikalottaram* into Telugu. His style was very simple and lucid. In addition to these translations, Pranavananda also wrote several original books, including *Ramana Maharshi Charitramu*, *Advaitabhoda Dipika*, *Tatwamali Dhyanamu*, *Sri Guru-Anugraha-avataramu*, *Dipamu Choodandi* and *Sri Ramana Stutipaatalu*.

For Pranavananda, spirituality was not mere intellectual exercise but the very way of life. From his childhood, he had great faith in the Rama Taraka mantram. He used to impart this mantram to his students, so that their hearts and their brains could acquire clarity and brilliance. He used to teach the Ramayana to his students, and they learned to appreciate and admire this priceless epic. One day, Bhagavan was sitting on the verandah with some devotees. Suddenly, a crow flew in at great

speed and fell at Bhagavan's feet. Bhagavan picked it up and
stroked its feathers gently. He saw that the crow was mortally
wounded, and tried to revive it, but it died in Bhagavan's lap.
"Some Siddha purusha has left his body today", said Bhagavan,
and gave instructions for entombing the dead crow.

While this was going on, Pranavananda came to the ashram.
Upon seeing him, Bhagavan said, "The entombment of the crow
is over." All the other devotees seemed to be impressed by the
gravity of the moment, but Pranavananda remained unmoved
and said to Bhagavan, "Why should Bhagavan expect us to be
impressed by this incident, as though it is some great achievement?
Is it really such a wonderful thing to have happened?" Everyone
was taken aback by Pranavananda's inexplicable reaction, but
Bhagavan remained grave and dignified.

Suddenly, Pranavananda broke into tears and said, "Why
Bhagavan, is this really a great deed that you have done now?
Did you not grant liberation to Jatayu in the last   yuga? Now
you have done the same for a crow. There is nothing strange
about this . . . it is just a routine affair for someone like you!"
Hearing this, the devotees were moved by Pranavananda's
devotion to Bhagavan, and his unshakable faith in Bhagavan's
divine nature. Bhagavan himself looked on silently, as though
he accepted everything.

Once, Pranavananda asked his grandson Hariprasad to
attend Bhagavan's *Jayanti* Celebrations. He instructed the boy to
get up early in the morning, have his bath and take his breakfast
with Bhagavan, and to leave immediately for *giripradakshinam*.
As the boy was about to leave, Pranavananda slipped a letter into
his pocket and told him to give it to Bhagavan.

Hariprasad followed his grandfather's instructions; he woke
up early in the morning and had his bath. Then he went and
prostrated to Bhagavan. Bhagavan made enquiries regarding

the welfare of all the family members, and told Hariprasad to have the iddlies and chutney that had been prepared for that day's breakfast. While he was eating, Hariprasad told Bhagavan that he wanted to set out on Giripradakshinam immediately after breakfast. Bhagavan said, "First of all, let me read the letter your grandfather has written to me", and he took the letter from the boy's pocket. Bhagavan asked for one more *idli* to be served to the boy, and read the letter while Hariprasad finished his breakfast. The letter contained the information that the Maharaja of Mysore was planning to visit Ramanasramam. Even though the boy had forgotten his grandfather's instructions, Bhagavan made sure that the letter was handed over to him.

Pranavananda had an ashram in Gudivada, in the Guntur District of Andhra Pradesh. However, he stayed in Vellore most of the time. Kulumani Narayana Sastri, a devotee of Bhagavan, also stayed in Vellore, and he was a close associate of Swami Pranavananda. He was devoted to both Bhagavan and to Seshadri Swami. Kulumani Sastri came to Bhagavan while Bhagavan was living on the Hill. At the very first meeting, he surrendered himself to Bhagavan.

There is an interesting story about Kulumani Sastri. It is as follows: Kulumani Sastri had written an abridged version of Valmiki's Ramayana in English prose. He wanted to have the first reading of the completed work, in Bhagavan's presence. Accordingly, he started up the Hill with his manuscript, and a big bunch of bananas as an offering for Bhagavan. On the way, he saw a Vinayaka temple and offered a few bananas from the bunch to Lord Vinayaka. This was done mentally; he did not actually remove the fruits from the bunch and leave them in the Vinayaka temple.

Kulumani Sastri went up the Hill and prostrated to Bhagavan, and laid the bunch of bananas before Bhagavan. The usual custom was for the attendant to put away all offerings safely, until they were distributed among the devotees, at an appropriate time. When the attendant came to remove the bananas, Bhagavan stopped him, saying that the fruits offered to Lord Vinayaka had yet to be removed from the bunch. The attendant and the other devotees were puzzled. Kulumani Sastri was stunned! He told the gathering that it was indeed true that he had mentally offered a few fruits to Lord Vinayaka on the way up the Hill, but had forgotten to separate those fruits from the bunch. Everybody was amazed at Bhagavan's omniscience.

Before Sastri even mentioned the purpose of his visit, Bhagavan himself said, "Sastri! Why don't you start reading the *Ramayana?*" Sastri was even more amazed than before! It was as though Bhagavan had photographed Sastri's mind and could see every detail in it.

One day, Pranavananda asked his grandson, Hariprasad, to fetch Kulumani Sastri. As soon as Sastri reached their house, Pranavananda asked him to recite *Rudra Namakam* and *Chamakam* along with him. At the end of this recitation, Pranavananda closed his eyes and repeated 'Hari Om'. With the Lord's Name on his lips, he merged with the divine. Thus ended Pranavananda's glorious life.

Pranavananda merged with Bhagavan in the year 1969, and his mortal remains were entombed on the banks of the River Palar, in Vellore. Though Pranavananda is no more with us, his memory lives on, through the numerous books he has written.